PRAISE FOR CONVERSATIONS WITH THE TAROT

"Whether you've had a long relationship with Tarot or you've just met, *Conversations with the Tarot* is a must-read. Equal parts mystical and practical, this book offers a unique perspective on the cards and how to achieve an intimate relationship with your deck. It is elegant and unexpected—a new classic for any Tarot devotee." ~ Deanna Raybourn, the New York Times bestselling author of the Veronica Speedwell series and tarot enthusiast

"Those of us who read Tarot often talk about "hearing what the cards have to say." Listening to the cards is the most vital part of our relationship with them. And Maria deBlassie listens deeply. In *Conversations with the Tarot*, she shares her experiences in lyrical, poetic language that encourages further exploration and deepens the reader's understanding of the Tarot, both as individual cards with messages to share and as a complex tapestry woven with the threads of the human experience. This book is moving and inspiring, well worth your time whether you're an old hand or new to Tarot." ~ Laura Perry, creator of *The Minoan Tarot* and author of *The Cryptic Guide to the Hopeless, Maine Tarot*

"Maria DeBlassie's Conversations with the Tarot is a beautifully written, inspiring, and insightful book. You could use it as a divination tool, as inspiration for your own journey, or to deepen your own tarot practice. There is a wealth of gentle wisdom here and compassionate insight, and I heartily recommend reading it." ~ Nimue Brown, author of *Pagan Dreaming* and *Beyond Sustainability*

Copyright © 2023 by Maria DeBlassie

All rights reserved. This book or any portion thereof may not be reproduced or used in any manner whatsoever without the express written permission of the publisher except for the use of brief quotations in a book review.

Edited by The Editing Hall and BZ Hercules

Cover Design by Rachel Ross Art

Published by Kitchen Witch Press

TYPO NOTE

Typos are the bane of any writer's existence. Like weeds, they pop up every time you think you're done with them.

It's easy to get irritated by this, but, when I'm not thinking of them as weeds, I'm seeing them as signs not to take myself too seriously. As Susanna Sturgis writes, "Typos are Coyote padding through the language, grinning." I have a healthy respect for Coyote, so I let him do what he will and grin with him.

If you should find a typo in my works, email me at mdeblassie@gmail.com and I will give you a free copy of one of my other publications.

CONTENTS

1. Introduction — 1
2. Ace of Wands Upright — 10
3. Insights — 11
4. The Knight of Swords Reversed — 12
5. Insights — 13
6. The Emperor Upright — 14
7. Insights — 15
8. Justice Upright — 16
9. Insights — 17
10. The Three of Cups Upright — 18
11. Insights — 19
12. The Four of Wands Reversed — 20
13. Insights — 21
14. The High Priestess Upright — 22
15. Insights — 23
16. The Page of Wands Upright — 24
17. Insights — 25
18. The Seven of Pentacles Reversed — 26

19.	Insights	27
20.	The Five of Pentacles Upright	28
21.	Insights	29
22.	The Knight of Cups Upright	30
23.	Insights	31
24.	The World Upright	32
25.	Insights	33
26.	The Six of Cups Upright	34
27.	Insights	35
28.	The Five of Swords Reversed	36
29.	Insights	37
30.	The Hermit Upright	38
31.	Insights	39
32.	The Seven of Cups Reversed	40
33.	Insights	41
34.	Temperance Reversed	42
35.	Insights	43
36.	The Ace of Pentacles Upright	44
37.	Insights	45
38.	The Two of Swords Reversed	46
39.	Insights	47
40.	The Eight of Wands Upright	48
41.	Insights	49
42.	Judgement Upright	50

43.	Insights	51
44.	The Three of Wands Reversed	52
45.	Insights	53
46.	The Two of Cups Reversed	54
47.	Insights	55
48.	The Knight of Pentacles Reversed	56
49.	Insights	57
50.	The Five of Cups Upright	58
51.	Insights	59
52.	The Lovers Upright	60
53.	Insights	61
54.	The Eight of Cups Reversed	62
55.	Insights	63
56.	The Hanged Man Upright	64
57.	Insights	65
58.	The Page of Swords Upright	66
59.	Insights	67
60.	The King of Wands Reversed	68
61.	Insights	69
62.	The Two of Wands Upright	70
63.	Insights	71
64.	The Ten of Wands Upright	72
65.	Insights	73
66.	The Ace of Swords Reversed	74

67.	Insights	75
68.	The Queen of Pentacles Reversed	76
69.	Insights	77
70.	The King of Pentacles Reversed	78
71.	Insights	79
72.	The King of Swords Reversed	80
73.	Insights	81
74.	The Four of Cups Reversed	82
75.	Insights	83
76.	The Two of Pentacles Upright	84
77.	Insights	85
78.	The Three of Swords Reversed	86
79.	Insights	87
80.	The Moon Upright	88
81.	Insights	89
82.	The Eight of Pentacles Reversed	90
83.	Insights	91
84.	The Six of Pentacles Upright	92
85.	Insights	93
86.	The King of Cups Upright	94
87.	Insights	95
88.	The Six of Wands Upright	96
89.	Insights	97
90.	The Hierophant Reversed	98

91.	Insights	99
92.	The Ten of Cups Upright	100
93.	Insights	101
94.	The Three of Pentacles Reversed	102
95.	Insights	103
96.	The Queen of Swords Reversed	104
97.	Insights	105
98.	The Page of Cups Upright	106
99.	Insights	107
100.	The Queen of Cups Reversed	108
101.	Insights	109
102.	The Nine of Swords Reversed	110
103.	Insights	111
104.	The Wheel of Fortune Upright	112
105.	Insights	113
106.	The Six of Swords Reversed	114
107.	Insights	115
108.	The Nine of Wands Reversed	116
109.	Insights	117
110.	The Fours of Pentacles Reversed	118
111.	Insights	119
112.	The Knight of Wands Reversed	120
113.	Insights	121
114.	The Seven of Swords Reversed	122

115.	Insights	123
116.	The Sun Reversed	124
117.	Insights	125
118.	The Fool Reversed	126
119.	Insights	127
120.	The Chariot Upright	128
121.	Insights	129
122.	The Devil Reversed	130
123.	Insights	131
124.	The Five of Wands Reversed	132
125.	Insights	133
126.	The Ace of Cups Upright	134
127.	Insights	135
128.	The Page of Pentacles Reversed	136
129.	Insights	137
130.	The Nine of Pentacles Reversed	138
131.	Insights	139
132.	The Star Upright	140
133.	Insights	141
134.	The Ten of Pentacles Reversed	142
135.	Insights	143
136.	The Queen of Wands Upright	144
137.	Insights	145
138.	The Nine of Cups Reversed	146

139.	Insights	147
140.	Death Reversed	148
141.	Insights	149
142.	The Eight of Swords Upright	150
143.	Insights	151
144.	The Magician Upright	152
145.	Insights	153
146.	Strength Upright	154
147.	Insights	155
148.	The Tower Upright	156
149.	Insights	157
150.	The Three of Pentacles Upright	158
151.	Insights	159
152.	The Seven of Wands Upright	160
153.	Insights	161
154.	The Ten of Swords Upright	162
155.	Insights	163
156.	The Four of Swords Upright	164
157.	Insights	165
158.	The Empress Upright	166
159.	Insights	167
160.	Conclusion	168
161.	About the Author	171

INTRODUCTION

When people think of the tarot, they think of mysterious fortune tellers and strange portents whispered under the watchful gaze of the full moon. They think of B horror movie foreshadowing, or the time they went with friends to a psychic late one night after a bad breakup and one too many drinks at the bar down the street. The tarot is, in other words, so commonplace it's almost a gothic story cliché and yet, for many, just otherworldly enough to feel out of reach in the daylight.

Me?

I just finished my morning cup of coffee and tarot draw. I like to pull a card first thing after I've completed my sunrise routine of making the bed, stretching out on my yoga mat, and feeding my familiar while listening to the news. My daily tarot pull has become part of that mundane ritual, a transition from the ephemeral just-woke-up to ready for the day's work—teaching or writing, depending on the day.

Sometimes I have a very specific question based on the events of the week or my sleep the night before. They can be follow-up questions to startling dream-time revelations, for example, or advice on a situation that doesn't seem to have a resolution in sight. Sometimes, my morning draw is simpler than that. I say "good morning" to the cards, shuffle the deck, and see what it wants to tell me. Other times, I'm seeking answers to a feeling—a vibe that I can't quite place and need insight on. Or an expected plot twist in my life so baffling, I just shuffle the deck and let my feelings, confusions, and thoughts on the matter flow through me and ask the tarot to comment on this situation and the energy surrounding it.

In other instances, the tarot comes to me.

A card falls from the deck as I shuffle, or I see the same card over and over again in my draws and randomly on social media, in books, in articles… The tarot wants to make sure I get the message. Sometimes, I even dream about it. It's as simple as seeing repeated tarot imagery in my dream life or as on the nose as literally dealing that tarot card in a vision.

In other words, the tarot has become such a mundane part of my life—part of my daily routine, my day-in, day-out, my witchy business—that it's magical. The tarot and I are one. We've developed our own bond over the years that only continues to grow and deepen as I work with it. And it is a partnership, a relationship developed on mutual respect and understanding, as strange as that may sound, unless you are someone who knows the power of bonding with a good book or a beloved jazz album. I don't tell the tarot what to do, and it doesn't tell me what to do (except, of course, if I keep bugging it, in which case it tells me to leave it alone and figure it out myself). Most of the time, we talk. It's a quiet conversation, like the kind I have with my familiar, the kind that involves a lot of listening and a lot of sensitivity.

You could say that the tarot is a lot like a cat: It doesn't like to be manhandled and it will only open up to you if you are willing to take time to get to know it. It won't be forced or rushed or told what to do. It also gets a little pissy if you try to coddle it too much. It has its own way of doing things, just like a cat, and it's best to go in with a healthy respect. If you do, well, then a pretty wonderful—and affectionate—relationship will follow.

So in other words, my understanding of the tarot has developed quite a bit since I started working with it. I, like so many others, once saw it as a mysterious occult artifact too often used as a prop in supernatural tales or the toolkit of highly trained mystical folks with deep knowledge of the esoteric realms. Now I see it as a wonderful everyday confidant, of sorts, that helps me tune in to my intuition and get insight into the world around me. And yeah, sometimes I use it in my stories to give ominous foreshadowing or gothic symbolism. Hey, the mystique is part of the joy!

The origin of the tarot, in fact, is as playing cards, and that mundane inception carried over into its more New Age reincarnation as a divination tool. Rather than being some sort of scary occult mystery, the tarot was designed to be accessible to everyday people interested in the mystic, which speaks to me deeply as a bruja who has always felt that true magic is in the everyday.

I've written whole books on the topic and center my whole mystic practice on that simple concept: everyday magic. It tells us that spirituality or the numinous isn't something outside ourselves that can only be found in formal arcane rituals or institutionalized religions but in something that is lived out in day-to-day life. The mystic is within us and a part of us, just as we are part of the natural world and the greater Universe. In fact, the more we align with this fundamental understanding, the more magical our lives become. Life unfolds as a waking dream, synchronicities abound, and we find the answers we need in life by simply attuning ourselves to the unseen world.

It's that simple. And that hard.

It takes a whole lot of trust and a whole lot of vulnerability to let go and open yourself to the subtle magic of the Universe. That's why the tarot can be helpful in getting perspective and cultivating our innate ability to know ourselves and the world around us. We live in a world that loves concrete, extroverted realities, not the quiet, soft things, the ephemeral things that sometimes can't be explained by words or logic.

In fact, that's how I first got into studying the tarot. I was looking for a way to deepen my spiritual practice. Sounds fancy, right? Roughly translated into everyday speak, I was looking to get perspective on my life and have more confidence in my own understanding of the world. I've always had solid instincts about people, places, situations, and what I've wanted out of my life. But then other people's viewpoints began to cloud my vision. Likewise, working in the world of academia could, when I wasn't sensitive enough to my own needs, dampen my gut feelings. Sometimes it still does. A college campus can be a wonderful place to grow and learn and teach. It can also be a place that can teach you to live inside your head if you're not careful. Life is a total body, mind, and spirit experience, and my journey into the tarot has been, in part, my journey into reconnecting to myself more holistically.

And like any good conjuring, exploring the tarot reminds us that the power is within us and all around us, not something that needs to be manufactured or forced. We just need to be open and receptive, then flow with the energy. There is much magic in opening ourselves to possibilities not yet imagined.

The tarot came to me at a time when I was beginning to open myself to those kinds of possibilities, exploring who I was outside of my day job. It was also an integral part of relearning my intuitive self, that internal voice, that gut reaction that told me all I needed to know about a situation. You know, the voice many of us so often silence or ignore because it runs counter to mainstream cultural values. And, as it happens, my tarot journey began with a wonderful act of synchronicity. It's an old superstition that you have to be gifted your first deck. That's not true—when you're ready to explore the tarot, simply find a deck that speaks to you. But in my case, that's exactly what happened—I was gifted my first deck, which was an important message to me to get going on my tarot studies.

I had literally been thinking that the tarot was something I wanted to explore. I hadn't told anyone about this desire, but it kept coming back to me in dreams, in synchronous social media posts featuring the tarot, in the display of tarot decks at my favorite metaphysical shops... It just kept popping up, kept speaking to me. Then, on my birthday, my parents gifted me with my first tarot deck, the Motherpeace tarot.

The message was clear: It was time to begin my tarot journey.

I started with the Motherpeace and, after a time, decided to seriously explore the Rider-Waite-Smith tarot, widely considered the standard deck in symbolism and iconography, so that I could understand the foundation of this form of divination. When I started, however, the whole thing felt daunting, like I was approaching some super important occult metaphysical thing. And, if I'm being honest, some of that was shaped by pop culture—the shows and movies that featured fortune tellers and mystics reading complex Celtic cross spreads and effortlessly unpacking the conversations the cards were having that correlated to very clear plot points in the story. (Fun fact: the tarot is rarely that transparent, but sometimes, uncannily, it can be—in retrospect.)

Still, I had felt like I needed a way to ground and focus my explorations and, being a writer as well as a bruja, journaling and scribbling will always be some of the most profound forms of conjuring for me. That's how my Tarot Tuesday project was born.

Starting in 2018, every week-ish (hey, I'm only human and the college semester being what it is, I took a break every now and then), I would draw from the deck, study the card, and write a 78-word story based on synchronicity and the conversation I had with the given card. 78 words for 78 cards in the tarot. I'd write about each card upright or reversed, however they presented themselves to me. There was much freedom in those imposed limits. Clear parameters allowed me to explore each card freely. With each post, I published my 78-word musing and a little bit of context, what I call Insights in this book, to explain how I was reading this card in the context of my studies, my daily life, and whatever synchronicity decided to add. For example, my plan was to only go through each card once, but the tarot had other ideas. In what can only be considered an act of trickster-worthy proportions, the Three of Pentacles reappeared almost a year after I had first written about it. Clearly, my deck felt I wasn't done with this card's wisdom during this project. This is something I've seen happen again and again as I've continued to converse with the tarot. The same card will continue to appear until I've internalized its message.

In the case of the Three of Pentacles, it first came to me reversed in the summer of 2019, at a time when I was learning there was such a thing as over-working or plodding along without getting the desired results. It's one thing to give it your all—and quite another to throw away time and energy on projects with diminishing returns. So, I used the wisdom of that card to get serious about the kind of work I wanted to do moving forward, work that was nourishing to both myself and my students but that didn't leave my inner well dry. I needed more time for replenishment and rest.

Close to a year later, after I thought I'd put the card aside in my "read" pile for this project, it appeared again, this time upright—a welcome reminder of how far I'd come in my efforts to create more work-life balance. While I still had a ways to go (this will no doubt always be a work-in-progress for me), I'd gotten to a point where I was better at applying myself to meaningful, fulfilling work that generated growth and excitement rather than depletion and burnout. I welcomed this synchronous reading from the tarot, especially since it occurred during the start of the pandemic and so much of my life felt topsy-turvy. The tarot swooped in to remind me that I'd grown more than I thought, and I wasn't as unmoored as I felt. What a relief!

I'll leave you with one more example of the magic that can happen when you develop your relationship with the tarot, one I didn't know existed until it hit me square in the third eye around the 2020 Spring Equinox and during week three of the first pandemic lockdown in New Mexico. I pulled the Queen of Wands, and in that card, I felt a deep affinity for who I was at my core—who I wanted to be again. She is a quietly gregarious person but also very much a figure who walks her own path and finds joy in living in her own way, on her own terms. And joyful she is, as sunshine and sunflowers surround her. My favorite part of the card, the one that spoke to me so deeply, is the little black cat sitting at her feet, front and center, boldly eschewing the superstition that black cats are bad luck. I, too, have a black cat, my familiar, who daily reminds me to walk my own path and find joy in the unexpected enchantments that come from nourishing my own vision of the world.

People think being an introverted rebel bruja means being isolated, salty, and anti-social. Frankly, how I'd been feeling with the burdens of the pandemic, even in its early stages, and the weight of the systemic oppressions and inequality that it magnified. But here was the Queen of Wands telling me on the Spring Equinox, a time for planting soul seeds and intentions, that being who I am is an act of joy, one that leads to meaningful connections and more than a little magic. I didn't have to fit in or toe the line. I didn't have to burn it all to the ground to make a meaningful change. I could be myself and find soul-nourishing solutions to my problems, ones that would allow me to live more deeply, more freely. Since our first meeting, the Queen of Wands regularly speaks to me. She is my affinity card, the one I most embody, the one that shades how I read the rest of the deck. She is hope, she is pleasure, she is joy—things we can all struggle to embody when the stresses of daily life get us down. Never fear, she reminds us, our capacity for joy is within us always; we just need to trust our instincts and embrace what makes us unique.

After two and a half years or so of devoting myself to this project, I'd gone through the whole tarot and had a much better understanding of how it worked. Perhaps more importantly, I'd bonded with my Rider-Waite-Smith deck and relearned fundamental aspects of myself, including how I wanted to be in the world, how I saw things. It also showed me that my instincts were spot on and that I could trust what I was feeling even without the cards. This project guided me through the wild waters of publishing my first book and, later, during the pandemic, showing me just how powerful the tarot can be when it comes to offering wisdom and insights as we navigate the good and the unexpected in our lives. But this study didn't make me an expert. I'm still very much a tarot novice. Can we ever really claim mastery over a topic that changes as we deepen our explorations?

As someone who has made a living doing research in one way or another, I've come to one solid conclusion: study only ever teaches us how little we know. And, I find, thanks to the ever-unfolding mysteries of the tarot, I'm quite all right with that. This project has led to the development of my *Bruja's Guide to Tarot*, where I show others how to begin their tarot journey and how to consult the deck to help us heal our relationship to hope, pleasure, and the magic of everyday life. But I would have never had the confidence in my own readings of the cards if I hadn't first explored them through my Tarot Tuesday project, which I have retitled *Conversations with the Tarot* for this book. I tell you this so that you can take comfort in knowing that none of us know what we're doing when we first start developing a relationship with the tarot but, in retrospect, we see patterns emerging in terms of how we read and understand the cards. A little time. A little attention. A little willingness to be vulnerable and look silly trying something new. It leads to a whole lot of magic!

This is very much a book about learning the tarot, and it's very much about encouraging those who find a resonance with the tarot to dive in and explore. But this isn't a book about how to do that. It's about the relationship you develop with the deck as you explore it. It's a meditation on the archetypes and the energy within it. It's about the art of conversing with the tarot and letting the revelations from those conversations unfold and develop as you would a chat with a good friend over a pot of tea.

It's likewise a study in how the tarot can really help us in our daily lives. When I started this project, I was beginning to return to my fiction writing and allowing myself to dream bigger about what my teaching career could look like. I ended this project in the middle of the first year of a global pandemic—certainly not something I was expecting when I started it. But the tarot was there to soothe and guide me even then, to offer me The Star when the pandemic first hit New Mexico. It was a soothing card, telling me it was time to pull inward, lean into our first lockdown, and really focus on self-care. So, this needed to be a time to reevaluate my life and shed anything that was holding me back. It also gave me a cosmic perspective, as The Star sees the whole of the Universe high up in the sky. The emotional distance to process an unprecedented situation that this card offered was a soothing balm to my heavy heart and frayed nerves in a situation where I felt very little emotional distance. So, you see, the tarot helped me through the various stages of the pandemic, guiding me to lean into this time of solitude rather than feed the panic and hysteria outside my sanctuary (a genuine privilege, I know, since I could work from home).

This book is also about keeping things simple. As I say in all my work, true magic is in the everyday. Translating that to my work with the tarot, all the 78-word stories and insights are about finding joy in our daily lives, starting by understanding that the mundane is magic. As for those Celtic cross readings… I'll never get to those in my tarot reading life. Sure, I suppose I could try them now and have done a few five and over spreads. Honestly? I still love the basic one- to three-card spreads. There is only so much I can absorb of the nuances of symbolism and, in my daily tarot conversations, I find there is much to unpack with just one card and the energy surrounding my question, depending on what is going on in my life at the time.

I have no real interest in getting too complicated about my readings. Similarly, I have no interest in reading for others. For me, the tarot is a private thing, the thing I turn to when I need a confidant, someone who can give me insights. But, as with any true confidant, it's important to know when to talk and when to trust yourself. You don't want to start looking to the tarot to be your Magic 8 Ball. It'll stop talking to you. Like a cat tired of being badgered by needy humans, it can and will walk away from you. The tarot is a confidant, sure, but not one you want to run to every time you're conflicted about something, lest you wear out your welcome. That's why I emphasize the conversational aspect of reading the tarot. It does not have magical answers for you or easy solutions. It merely offers you some insights and, with luck, helps you better trust your own instincts.

What's more, learning the fluid synchronous study of the tarot with the Rider-Waite-Smith deck has allowed me to freely explore other decks, even oracle cards, and given me more confidence in developing my own readings and interpretations of the cards. The more you study the tarot, the more you learn that, while there might be general card meanings, the nuances and variety of interpretations are as vast and unique as the readers themselves. We each have a different way of engaging with the tarot, each a different lens for perceiving the world around us.

I always tell beginning tarot explorers that they should choose the deck and their readers synchronously, feeling their way through the energies that most resonate with them because that energy, be it via a deck or professional reader, will be just the kind of magic and insight they need. You'll notice that I can't seem to write about a card without drawing on the imagery of seeds, growing things, books and stories, sunlight, and the homey delights of introverts. That's because I'm an introverted bruja who loves a spot of kitchen witchery or puttering about my magical garden when I'm not writing stories or conversing with my familiar. See? I can't interpret the tarot without drawing on my experience of life as I've known it.

Which brings us to this book... and why you're reading it. I'm a big believer in book magic, that alchemical process of finding a book, or having a book find you, just when you need it. Vibes match up, synchronicity gets to work, and suddenly, you're perusing a book whose wisdom you didn't know you needed. Yet, here we are. If you've found this book, it means it has some medicine for you. Whether you are a beginning tarot explorer or a long-time practitioner wanting to reconnect with the everyday magic of your tarot practice, this book is a useful study in finding the subtle enchantments in this mundane form of divination.

This book is set up chronologically, starting with my first pull of the deck so many years ago and ending with the very last one. I have my 78-word story, which I think of as spells, or my impressions of the card, at the top of the page, and the Insights right after it. These proverbial spells are meant to invoke a feeling or sense of wonderment for the moments in our lives when the mundane and the mystic overlap—so, like, every minute of every day if we attune ourselves to this magic. That's spell work at its deepest: understanding how words build our world, how language shapes our reality, and how, through the simple act of voicing something or committing pen to paper, can we conjure magic in our daily lives. So mote it be, and all that.

The Insights after these proverbial spells are designed to offer a deeper reading of the card and why I chose to write the story or study that I did. The Insights offer life contexts as well, exploring how the meaning of each card is shaped by what we're going through day-to-day. I modeled this organization after texts like *The Unseen Partner: Love & Longing in the Unconscious,* a powerful study of one woman's journey into Jungian psychology through the lens of art, poetry, and scholarship. I was also inspired by Jenna Moore Fuller's books, especially *The Secret Language of Synchronicity: Deciphering the Words & Wisdom of Meaningful Coincidence,* which delves into her personal experience with synchronicity as a way to encourage others to explore this secret and magical language.

And speaking of book magic, let's talk about the best way to approach reading this book. Like I said earlier, it's not a traditional how-to book, but rather an exploration of how the tarot comes alive through storytelling and contemplation. You can read it straight through, from start to finish, marinating in the mystic wisdom of a card a day, or you can you use this book as a form of mundane divination in its own right. Simply hold the book, think of a question, situation, or feeling, and when you feel ready, open the book to a random page. There, you will find the magic you need.

As life changes around us, the tarot is there to guide us, offer us insight, and help us better listen to our heart of hearts. As you'll see, the way I read the tarot is all about how it can help us heal our relationship to hope, pleasure, and the magic of everyday life.

Are you ready to begin your tarot journey?

ACE OF WANDS UPRIGHT

Another stormy afternoon. You deal the deck
by candlelight. Time for new stories. You
ask the lightning for a lick, just a taste
of its spark. It gives you a fire
seed that won't wait for you to plant
it. The wind takes care of it for you, blowing
on that sliver of light and pushing
it into the unknown. And the card in your hand,
like a promise, asks only that you open
yourself to the elements.

INSIGHTS

At the time I drew this—my first tarot card—I couldn't help feeling it was an auspicious beginning to my Tarot Tuesday project! I drew the upright Ace of Wands one rainy afternoon and the message was clear: don't wait. Forge ahead with your new project and let the rest follow. The aces are always about bright potential and fresh starts. They are pure inspiration, asking you to push aside doubt and dive into life. They may not be fully formed but contain the essence of everything you need on your new journey. All you have to do is trust the bright, positive energy of this card in its upright position. I guess I was on the right path with this new project!

The Ace of Wands is like a seed—pure potential, no guarantees. You have to take the initiative, plant it, tend the new energy or idea you're working on to see them blossom. You also have to ignore your fears and self-doubt, the killers of creative wand energy and ace inspirations. You don't have to have all the answers or completely know what you're doing. It's the getting started that matters.

THE KNIGHT OF SWORDS REVERSED

Your light blazes a trail, forgetting that it's not just
dead leaves and sticks that it gobbles
up. The ground moves too quickly
beneath you. Your flame spreads
too thin, threatening to smoke
out birds from their nests and
singe innocent dandelions. You rein
in your wild thoughts. Collect
your light. Enjoy the feel
of it around you like a golden blanket,
nourishing rather than all-consuming. You
don't always have to be the warrior.
Just soft light.

INSIGHTS

When I drew the Knight of Swords, reversed, as the second installment of my Tarot Tuesday project, I was feeling tired from multiple commitments and thinking of adding even more to my plate. Then this card revealed itself to me. Go slow, it said. Don't go charging straight ahead without taking in your surroundings and becoming aware of the potential issues that might arise from blindly going forward. This reversed action-oriented card (as all knights are), asked me to focus my energy so that it doesn't become scattered, diluted. It reminded me to try going it alone for a bit, to get my bearings rather than moving too fast. Burnout is real, and I needed to give myself permission to rest and allow my latest writing and life inspirations to unfold at a gentler pace.

The Knight of Swords is very much a card that asks, "What's the rush?" We can be fueled by excitement, anxiety, or a sense of obligation to just keep going and doing more at the expense of our mental, physical, and spiritual well-being. See the horse in this image? He doesn't look too good. The knight is literally running the beast into the ground, showing how this sort of internalized pressure to "keep going" can be a way of beating up on ourselves or expecting too much from ourselves. The better way to go about things—the healthier way—is to slow down, take a good look at what's behind this obsessive drive to keep doing more and learn the art of being gentle, deliberate, and slow in our movements, intentional in our actions.

THE EMPEROR UPRIGHT

I am sovereign to no one
but myself. Ruler of a world
shaped by bones, wrapped
in skin, flowing with crimson
stories. I export these tales
to other realms, a fair trade:
stories for sustenance. Medicine
in curves and folds of written
words for both scribbler
and the healing soul. I send
them away, but they never
leave. They flow back to me
when I least expect it.
They are my heart. Without
them, I have no compass.

INSIGHTS

When the Emperor appeared to me that day, I thought about sovereignty, our ability to do what we need to do in the world, be who we need to be, and the power of claiming our ability to bring the things we've dreamed up into the waking world. Of course, as a writer, I have to acknowledge what a huge influence stories and storytelling have on me, so much so that my beloved books and narratives often feel like they rule over me, guiding me on my path when I can't see the forest for the trees. When I drew this card, I was also thinking about what it takes to birth my first book. *Everyday Enchantments* is the physical manifestation of my intuitive magic, as is all my writing. And it takes a certain amount of strength, focus, and structure (all characteristics of the Emperor card) to conjure these written spells and release them into the world. This card reminded me that I was more than capable of doing it.

The Emperor is part of the major arcana, or the suit of the tarot reserved for the big-picture archetypal energies that influence your life. These cards are always about life lessons and destiny. Although I often talk about goddess energy, the divine feminine, and the often undervalued significance of traditionally feminine interiority, it is equally important to acknowledge the power of the divine masculine or the healthy assertion of self in the world (not to be confused with toxic masculinity, which works against, not with, the sacred feminine). This is an extroverted card, the yang to introversion's yin, in which the Emperor rules in a way that ensures the happiness and well-being of his kingdom. It was an interesting card to get right around Father's Day, too, the ultimate celebration of sacred masculinity.

JUSTICE UPRIGHT

Balance is restored. Each seed, each choice weighed
and tasted until Karma speaks her truth, your law. You called
to her, begging for answers, and she appeared in your stolen
pocket of solitude, though surely you wouldn't be punished
for that thievery. Who suffers? None. And who heals? The bruised
heart finding its way in the world. You offer it to her, one more story
to add to the scales. Her sword slices a clear path into discovery.

INSIGHTS

Ahhh... the Justice card literally deals with law and order, but not always in the way we think. This is the karma card, the card that restores balance and sets things to right. Typically, we think of it in terms of someone "getting what they deserve," a statement that can have a negative connotation. But karma is really all about understanding how the energy you put out into the world affects you and your life. We make decisions, walk down certain roads, and life happens.

After enough bumps, twists, and turns, we get a sense of how our actions shape our journey. This card always asks you to consider your cosmic karma and how you can find a way to be truer to yourself. The androgynous Libra won't let you hide from hard truths or tough decisions. They are impartial, more concerned about psychic or cosmic law than the minutia that makes up our lives. When the Justice card walks into your life, it is asking you to take stock, restore balance, and learn the lessons you need to learn so that you can move forward in your life with clarity and purpose.

THE THREE OF CUPS UPRIGHT

It's over. Finally. And in its place are flowers
and wine and golden cups that never
run dry. They are full of liquid stories that purify
bruised hope and protect newly blossoming
hearts. Here is beauty in bare feet kissing
the earth. Here is joy in the laurel's cradled arms. Taste
it. Trust it. Revel in it. Let your hair
down and dance, get drunk on the elixir
of life, and remember
what it means to begin again.

INSIGHTS

Sometimes it just feels so good to be at the end of something! To feel that what you've been struggling with has reached its natural conclusion, and to know that in its place is joy, abundance, hedonism. Such is the wisdom of the Three of Cups Upright. The threes in the minor arcana more generally represent unifying forces, things coming together to generate new life. The cups represent emotional intelligence and intuition. This is a cleansing card, focusing on harmonious relationships with self and others, and the promise of good times.

THE FOUR OF WANDS REVERSED

My world is upside
down. Roots are shaggy
about my head. My feet dance
in the sky. I've planted so many seeds,
but for every one that bears fruit, many
others are blown away, eaten by birds
or simply never born. But
they weren't meant to sprout. They weren't
my stories to live out. So where
do I go from here? I will pause. I will
delight. I will taste tomatoes, bursting
sweet and juicy across my tongue.

INSIGHTS

The Universe has a way of making us face our truths, whether we want to or not. Sometimes they are pleasant, and sometimes they knock us for a loop! In either case, they are always meant to help us live in better alignment with our true selves. In traditional readings, reversed cards can have "negative" connotations, but this is the tarot, after all, which means we have to think poetically. In this case, the Four of Wands reversed is about the bumps and blocks that can hit after a big revelation. There's the initial awe and liberation at your new understanding, and then the worry sets in. Can I move forward into deeper consciousness? Am I ready for this much freedom? This much joy? The answer, of course, is always YES! This card asks you to pause and honor the transition you now find yourself in. Let go of old ways, let go of your ego that wants things a certain way, at a certain time. Instead, celebrate the fact that you've allowed yourself to see what you needed to see. The fours in the tarot are all about stability and the focusing of energy, while the wands are all about fire energy. In essence, this card, even reversed, is asking you to get grounded, get real—but still enjoy yourself.

THE HIGH PRIESTESS UPRIGHT

Do not fear her darkness. Only let her slip
pomegranate seeds between your lips so
that you may savor the bits of your soul you
are just beginning to birth. Learn the taste
of yourself. Be swallowed by her shadows and moonlight
just as you swallow her ruby wisdom. Discover
your path is in stardust and radish roots. That you
are sacred. You don't need maps to illuminate
the way into the underworld. It is an old road.

INSIGHTS

This card is all about the divine feminine. We get caught up in life, keeping up with the proverbial Joneses, thinking we should be living in a certain way, or looking for concrete answers to metaphysical questions. The High Priestess asks you to trust your magic. There is a cosmic law out there that needs you to trust the Universe and your own soul. Forget logic, forget the waking world. This is a card whose magic comes from symbols, dreams, the underworld, the unconscious. Like Persephone descending into the underworld, the High Priestess can travel between realms to discover the most profound divine revelations. She is one with herself and one with the world in all its aspects. She can also signal change, as drawing her card illuminates what you hadn't previously been willing to see. And with revelation comes transformation.

THE PAGE OF WANDS UPRIGHT

Remind me what morning sunshine tastes
like before I needed coffee to savor it. Brush
the dust from my heart, so I can marvel
at the way it beats. Feed me watermelon, barefoot
together in the grass, because it tastes
the sweetest that way. Allow
me to dream without bounds so that I forget to fence
in my wild thoughts or fear that the wishes
I cast to the sky won't come true. The right ones always do.

INSIGHTS

This card is brought to you by my little niece, who actually pulled the Page of Wands just one day before we got to meet her new cousin. Normally, the tarot is poetic, cryptic, making us work for answers, so we move beyond the literal and delve into the realm of imagination. This time around, though, it was pretty darn specific. One of the readings of the card is that a new person is about to enter our lives. This person might seem a little immature at first (say, like, five months old, maybe?) but is a true and sincere person and a force for good in your life. So, the cards were literally preparing my three-year-old niece for the arrival of a new family member!

Of course, there's always the poetic side too. The Page of Wands, like all pages, represents childlike wonder and the vibrant energy of youth. It's an invitation to dream big and dive into a new creative project, or to develop an emerging side of yourself. It's all about reclaiming your natural innocence as you move forward. The wands, likewise, are about new inspiration, primal energy unfettered by intellect or the daily grind. This card asks you to stay playful, see the world from the awe and wonder of a newborn, and enjoy the new path you find yourself on.

THE SEVEN OF PENTACLES REVERSED

The moon went dark. The shadows crawled out
from under the rocks where they'd been hiding and spread
out before you like so many empty promises. When had you given
so many of them a home to squat in? No wonder
you've felt short on space. Cramped. Like you couldn't fully stretch
your wings. It's time for them to go. You let the reemerging lunar light
sweep them away like specks of dust. Then you prepare for flight.

INSIGHTS

Have you ever been in a situation where you pour your heart and soul into something, or maybe just expend a lot of energy, hoping that the time and attention you put into it will be rewarded, then discover that the opposite is true? It wasn't the magical thing you thought. It was draining you, taking more than it was giving. We've all been there—whether it's a situation, place, or relationship—and sooner or later, we get to a point where we realize it's not worth the effort. Or that we need to adjust our expectations. This can be in big ways (leaving toxic situations) or small ways (an attitude adjustment).

It can feel disheartening, at first, to know you've given so much, only to throw in the towel. But the truth is, it's incredibly healthy and energizing to recognize when you're expending energy inappropriately. The Seven of Pentacles in reverse asks us to look for places where we are expending energy without compensation, where we are wasting our time, and to cut the dead weight loose. Only then can we reclaim our energy and move forward in more positive, generative ways.

This card was an interesting draw on the heels of the lunar eclipse, which literally lays bare stagnant energy so that we can clear through it and let go of the things weighing us down. So when we think of transformation, we think of butterflies and sparkles, but it's also hard work. It's acknowledging things we need to let go of. This card reversed gives us permission to let go, move on, and nourish only what brings us joy, health, and abundance.

THE FIVE OF PENTACLES UPRIGHT

Winter snakes cold, bony fingers around
your body, reminding you that you miss four walls
and a door closed against harsh elements, a cozy
fire and an overstuffed chair to drink tea in. But you
aren't sure you have enough strength
to make it into that sanctuary. Not until you hobble
into a pool of light, a stained-glass kiss
on an otherwise dark night. It is enough to spur you
forward, enough to light your way home.

INSIGHTS

Want to throw things for a loop? Draw one of the fives in the tarot. They are the rebels, forever wanting to shake up the status quo, push us out of our comfort zones, and turn things topsy-turvy. Most upright cards in the tarot are considered positive, while the reversed are negative. Not so for the fives. They like to do things their own way. Upright fives often indicate something "bad" (I use quotes there because even when the tarot reveals something negative, it is always with the positive intention of healing and transformation). Usually, they want you to consider how your reliance on the status quo limits your ability to think outside the box. This, in turn, leads to stagnation and unhappiness.

Things get even more interesting when you pair this transgressive number with the pentacles, which are all about stability. Literally speaking, they are about finances... But this is the tarot, after all, so we need to remember to think a little more metaphorically about this. This suit in the minor arcana always addresses prosperity in all its forms: emotional, spiritual, physical, and financial. So we have a number of rebellion paired with a suit of stability. The Five of Pentacles is a card about feeling left out in the cold. Here's my more poetic take on this, courtesy of an old witchy saying: as within, so without.

In essence, the Five of Pentacles can indicate spiritual poverty or disconnection from our inner selves. This happens for all sorts of reasons. We give out too much to people, trying to help them or fix things that are not ours to fix. We over-extend ourselves, hoping that energy, money, and attention will give us the desired results (again, one of those formulas the fives asks us to shake when we stop seeing a return on our energetic investment). Sometimes, we even accidentally stir up old ghosts that make us doubt ourselves as we move forward with our lives. Fear not, however, as the fives only reveal discord to remind you that you have the power to set things right. For even as you might feel disconnected from yourself, there is always a light—symbolized in the card by the stained-glass window—that guides us back to ourselves.

THE KNIGHT OF CUPS UPRIGHT

I think I'm being rescued. Yet
instead of sword and steel, my knight
wears a helmet made of daisy heads
and lavender buds. His armor
is chain-linked poetry
whereas mine has been
stripped from me like tin petals. He
offers me not another battle
but a golden cup filled
with honeyed wine. Sees
each of my scars as the promise
of a good story. Vows divinity
in his fiery embrace. I feel I'm
developing a taste for salvation.

INSIGHTS

I'll be honest. In my youth, I was never much for knights in shining armor, mostly because I was too busy slaying my own dragons to wait around for someone to rescue me. Over the years, however, I've learned the value of said knights and of being rescued—a bit of playful wisdom that comes, strangely, from maturity. I mean, who doesn't want to be swept off their feet once in a while? In fact, I've come to see being swept off your feet, rescued by a guardian angel, or knocked for a loop by the trickster messenger god Hermes himself, as a necessity of life. It keeps things playful and passionate!

Such is the wisdom of the Knight of Cups upright. This knight is a lover, not a fighter, slowly but surely moving forward in his pursuit of romance and divine creativity. This is very much a card about tuning into the romance of life. After all, if you've been busy slaying dragons, you can sometimes forget that there's more to life than kicking ass (although that's pretty cool too). This knight is ruled by his heart and intuition and is no less fierce than the other knights in the minor arcana. He is just as focused and valiant in his seductive efforts as those other knights are in their battle cries. It's just that this knight wants to remind you that your hopes and dreams are coming to fruition, that you will soon experience divine relief from a long worried-over problem, and, of course, that romance is in the air—however you choose to define love. The Knight of Cups rescues us from stagnation and old woes and, more importantly, of feeling like we always need to be warriors. Now it's time to let the love in.

THE WORLD UPRIGHT

I hold in my hand a map of the world. My
world. The rivers are made of sweeping
prose, and the land, lush alphabets
begging to be touched. Each of the apples
in the orchard holds a story that can only be
experienced by biting into willing flesh
underneath a shady grove. So much
time and care given to helping a seed sprout,
blossom, plant roots, and flourish
into a life-giving tree. The fruits,
however? Eternal. Delicious.

INSIGHTS

I love jazz music, and, after listening to some great live jazz before drawing this card, I found myself humming the old classic "I've Got the World on a String." Although, in reality, that thought felt a little too glib for what I'd been feeling that week. It was less "I've got the world on a string" and more like I've finally found my place in it. I felt like I was one with the Universe and happy with the life I've carved out for myself... which is exactly what The World in the tarot represents. This is the final card in the major arcana representing fulfillment and cosmic completion. The Fool has reached the end of her journey and is rejoicing in newfound happiness and success.

It can also represent a long-worked-for achievement coming to fruition, and I can't help but think of my first book, *Everyday Enchantments*, in regard to this reading, as I'd just been putting some things together for the fall release right before drawing this card. It had been six years of hard work, much of it spent quietly writing without anyone noticing or caring. I was incredibly excited to see my first book in print.

Such is the wisdom of The World. It reminds us that we've overcome many obstacles, put in many long hours, committed so much energy to see our hard work rewarded at last. It's time to rejoice and celebrate hard-earned accomplishments and begin tending to new dreams, new projects, new adventures.

THE SIX OF CUPS UPRIGHT

Outside the window of my childhood
bedroom was an oasis. At its center
was a cherry tree. It gave me blush-stained
flowers in the spring and fat, tart cherries
in the summer. Fall was for orange flames
flickering, then sputtering to the ground. So it was,
until one year, the naked branches of winter stayed
on through spring, then summer, and the tree
was no more. Gone, except for a love
of cherry pie on a warm night.

INSIGHTS

In the midst of change, big or small, we can find ourselves looking to the past for comfort, reflection, and wisdom. I always find myself with an effusion of back-to-school memories come fall as I get ready to begin teaching after a restful and rejuvenating summer off. I want to sharpen pencils, despite the fact that I do my grading online now. I want to organize my backpack even though I no longer own one, and I get excited about planning my first day of school outfit because, well, some things don't change. Similarly, not a summer goes by that I don't crave cherry pie, thanks to the many wonderful memories of harvesting cherries from the tree in my family's backyard to make this homey dessert.

Such is the story behind the Six of Cups. The sixes bring welcome relief and sanctuary after the upheaval and discord of the fives. It is comforting, a coming home of sorts. Just avoid the pitfalls of nostalgia, and instead, relish the past that brought you to this present moment. The Six of Cups can also indicate that you need to get in touch with your inner child, and to create space for child-like wonder and joy, without filter or censorship.

THE FIVE OF SWORDS REVERSED

I've clashed swords over kingdoms and
pride and broken promises. I've fought
for my life, and I've fought to keep
my soul intact. I've done this so many times, I
begin to realize the field before me could be so
much more than muddied gore. I
am done with this. I turn away, fashioning my sword
into a shovel that will transform this beaten
earth into a garden. Sometimes the battle
is in knowing when to let go.

INSIGHTS

The fives are up to their old tricks again, making the upright negative and the reversed... something of a cathartic revelation. The Five of Swords reversed signals that there is a large conflict that's about to be resolved, mostly because you're tired of dealing with it. It's either a peaceful resolution or a case where you simply throw in the towel, knowing when to cut your losses and move on. Forget about things that aren't yours to fix. Forget about making everything work. Sometimes, you just need to let old wounds finally heal, let go of battles that aren't yours to fight, and focus your energies on what brings joy and wellness into your life.

THE HERMIT UPRIGHT

There is a lantern inside my chest. I am
only just beginning to know the flicker
and wave and luminosity of it. I need
time. Time to taste red, yellow, orange. Time
to know what keeps it burning without
consuming me or dwindling into a spent ember.
I marvel at the way it lights my path, though it only offers
me one golden footprint at a time. No matter. It is enough
to take the next deliberate step.

INSIGHTS

True confession time: Every time fall rolls around, I find myself looking forward to the simple routines of this more introverted season. It's kind of like when someone cancels plans with you, and you're secretly relieved and excited that you get to stay home and drink tea and read books. Not because you don't want to see that person, but because you are craving some much-needed introvert time. That was my vibe when I pulled this card (okay, and most of the time). I often pine for quiet evenings and the simple routine of teaching, writing, and cultivating the simple pleasures of gardening, cooking, reading, and now, tarot reading.

Yet sometimes I feel a little guilty or bad about these desires. Let's face it, in an extroverted world, being an introvert always feels a little transgressive. Is there something wrong with me? Is it okay if I take time for myself? Should I be doing more stuff... with more people? But in my heart of hearts, I know that what I truly need after a week of extroverted teaching is quiet time alone or with close loved ones.

I want to read. I want to write. I want to lose track of time in the garden.

Such were my thoughts when I drew The Hermit. I was shuffling the deck, letting the cards pick up my vibe, as is my routine, when an introspective figure holding a lantern caught my eye. *Hmm... that would be an interesting card to explore when the time came*, I thought and continued to shuffle. After several minutes, I spread out the cards facedown across my desk and chose one a little hidden under the others at the end of the spread. I flipped it over and came face-to-face with The Hermit, the same card that caught my eye while I was shuffling.

The message was clear. Not once, but twice, the tarot spoke to me of the divine power of turning inward. It's okay to take time for yourself. It's okay to relish solitude and nourish your inner life.

THE SEVEN OF CUPS REVERSED

There are so many options. Each cup I drink
from can offer me so much. Yet, I can't possibly sip
from each one. Don't want to. I part the clouds, looking for the cup
that will quench my thirst. It calls to me, like a siren
song, though I know I'm in no danger
as I open my heart to it. There it is, filled with ink and bone
and stories and blood. At last, I am satiated.

INSIGHTS

This card is all about getting grounded and reassessing your priorities. In reverse, this card asks you to consider how to make your dreams a reality and to focus on what makes you truly happy. It gives you permission to consolidate your energy, pull in, and take only what will truly fulfill you, while leaving the rest.

It's an intuition card, asking you to trust your gut and inner wisdom despite any insecurity or anxiety that crops up. A very helpful card since I pulled it when my first book, which is basically pieces of my soul written in ink for all the world to see, was almost out. Sure, nothing to get nervous about at all. But the Universe spoke to me and told me to stay steady, trust my dreams, and not be afraid to bring them into the waking world.

What dreams do you want to bring to fruition? How will you tend your inner landscape so that you are ready to conjure?

TEMPERANCE REVERSED

Noise, so much noise. You worry your voice
isn't strong enough to hear over
the din. Perhaps it is not the noise
that's the matter; you must leave this loud
place behind. You go into the woods
and find the deepest darkest cave and descend. Past
the rocks and pools of water. Past the dangling
roots and old forgotten stories. You
find your home in the darkness. You
find your home in the silence. There is your voice.

INSIGHTS

This was the third week in a row that the cards told me to go low and slow, turn inward, and enjoy the sweetness of quiet time. Temperance reversed is a card that speaks of imbalance and the need to find your way back to soul, back to self. It's easy to want to fill up your time and keep moving. We live in a world that loves fast and easy, so it can be tempting to stay on the surface of things. However, autumn, when I drew this card, is the season of descending into the underworld, like Persephone, turning inward and taking time to reconnect with ourselves. Nothing says autumn like nourishing your inner life.

When Temperance reversed comes into your life, it is asking you to pause and listen to yourself. Maybe you've been overdoing it in one way or another or not giving yourself time to rest, or you've simply got a lot on your plate. A little solitude here will help you work through old selves and self-doubts that crop up when you're depleted or feel that your inner and outer world are out of balance. This card also reminds you that you know what you need to do to heal yourself. The reversal of this card suggests that your healing will always be deeply personal and private, as all good magic is.

THE ACE OF PENTACLES UPRIGHT

You have a pocket full of gold coins
made of aspen leaves and a stack of greens
after seasons of sowing seeds. There is a gateway
in your garden, made of morning glories and old stories.
Just beyond that gateway—the taste of adventure. You
feel it in the ground, the dark soil and rocks
sifting through your fingers. You taste it in the breeze, begging
to wrap itself around you. This, this is yours. Of your making.

INSIGHTS

Wow, after weeks of the tarot telling me to go low and slow and find my center, I got the Ace of Pentacles. It's time for new beginnings and a flood of positive energy. This card always signals abundance in all things. This prosperity is truly powerful because it is grounded in your hard work and union with the earth. It's about stability and security as much as it's about wealth, in all senses of the term. This card is especially powerful to me because it is about working in harmony with nature. The gate featured in the card's image is made of foliage seamlessly crafted out of the surrounding greenery. When this card comes into your life, it means you are achieving long-worked-for prosperity. And there is something waiting just beyond the gate: a new adventure, an extra dash of spice to this bucolic scene, another delicious opportunity for who knows what!

THE TWO OF SWORDS REVERSED

Windy fingers wind themselves around
my sweater, trying to pull me from home. Insisting
I follow a road offering me nothing but bricks
other people wish I'd walk on. Don't they know I need
bare earth under my feet? That's a conversation
for another day. Today, I find peace in the warm
glow of my kitchen. I slice apples. I roll out dough. I make pie,
letting cinnamon and solitude perfume
my home. For now, it is enough.

INSIGHTS

When I first drew the Two of Swords reversed, it spoke to me of the in-between spaces I feel most at home in. Liminal spaces that ask us to question straight and narrow paths or ways of thinking, or our riding attempt to have all the answers to all the things right now. This is very much a card of making peace with the journey, rather than the destination. It's about enjoying our time in limbo and taking time to pull in and find our balance between our inner needs and the outer demands of the world.

So I drew the card, learned about the card, and sat down to write my 78-word story... and once again found myself in a state of in-between. The story was almost done, but not quite. I needed something—time—to get it just right, so I had to make my peace with letting it marinate. Here was a card speaking of balance, limbo, and unfinished things. Here I was with an unfinished Tarot Tuesday post that was unlikely to be completed that week. I made my peace with it. I also made pie. And I took the time the tarot asked me to so I could be in better balance with the inner and outer way of things, at home in the liminal space where magic and grace are found.

THE EIGHT OF WANDS UPRIGHT

There is a fire inside me. A blue flame in the center
of my chest, just below my ribcage. It tells me I can handle
the storm, carve the new path, even sit beside the candle's
light and rest. It dances and sparkles and lights
the way. A stray spark here, daring me
to say no to an adventure. A burst of flame—
the promise of another story. The bend and wiggle
against the wind: a hedonistic dance.

INSIGHTS

Buckle up and enjoy the ride—that's the message of the Eight of Wands. Whenever this card enters your life, it's a time of high-powered, free-flowing, creative inspiration. Don't hold back, like we are sometimes tempted to do in the midst of overwhelming energy, good or bad. The eights in the tarot are all about strength, accomplishments, and focused energy. The wands are vessels of primal energy, wild and wanton like fire. Combine this fiery passion with the solidity of the eights, and you've got a powerhouse of positive energy from within making its way into the outer world.

JUDGEMENT UPRIGHT

I stand at the crossroads holding
lint and a handful of admonishments, heavy
like stones. Why did I keep these when I'd tossed
my embroidered flowers and paper birds? Foolish
mistakes. Then the road reminds me I'm not the flower
or the bird or even the lint, but a woman whole
with an open road spread before her. I need only
a pocketful of seeds and this golden
leaf in my open palm—a gift from the aspen.

INSIGHTS

The Judgement card is less judgy-judgy and more about getting real about who you are and what makes you happy—and what doesn't. This card is like a call to level-up cosmically. Know thyself, trust thyself, and allow thyself to move forward without old self-doubts or regrets holding you back. Let go of all that baggage and embrace a new, hard-worked-for way of being. This card isn't about subtlety—it literally features the Angel Gabriel calling you to embrace your inner divinity. So do it! Find your inner goddess or divinity, listen to her, and let her guide you. Nothing else matters.

THE THREE OF WANDS REVERSED

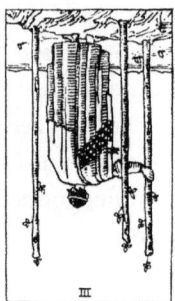

All I need is the dirt road with enough space
to plant my feet. I can figure out the rest as I go.
Then I start thinking I need bricks and mortar
to pave the way, as if stones in the ground
would make my road easier. The gossiping
trees dotting the road are my saviors, whispering
that buried blocks only clog the path. The sky
and birds agree, showing me
how beautiful it is to be weightless.

INSIGHTS

The Three of Wands reversed is about embracing the bumps in the road and knowing intrinsically that they are there to bring you back to yourself. These setbacks can make you feel like you wasted your time, but we are in the realm of tarot and magic, after all, so that is never the case. These blockages are always messages from Trickster Coyote, guiding you back to yourself and your own path. You remember who you are and what you stand for. You remember what brings you joy and lights up your life. This card is all about embracing the magic that comes from these curveballs and moving forward with the creative insight and inspiration they conjure.

THE TWO OF CUPS REVERSED

I crave the connection. Large hands
cradled around a ceramic mug. Cinnamon
and orange rinds perfuming
the water, steam tickling my nose. I want
to be that cup—full. Brimming with joy. Overflowing
with so much heat, it births golden crystals to freckle
the red clay it's made from. Held by gentle fingers
and capable hands. Warming as I am warmed.
Filling as I am filled. Tasting of clove and sweet
things. Just bring me to your lips.

INSIGHTS

The Two of Cups reversed practically begs you to take some self-care time. This card reversed is all about loving yourself unconditionally. It reminds you that you've fallen out of balance, out of tune with your natural rhythms and inner life, and that you need to reconnect to the love and positive vibes the Universe is sending your way. The lovers in this card, along with the lion overseeing their union, ask you to go boldly and passionately toward what makes your heart sing, without apology or hesitation. In essence, this card wants you to take time to regroup, care for yourself, and take some time to consider what truly makes you happy.

THE KNIGHT OF PENTACLES REVERSED

Snow is on the ground, a blank
slate I want to run
my feet and fingers over. I
need to do something. Anything. Feel
compelled to see movement
across the crystal landscape.
In the stillness, I see it: the
lone robin picking its way across
a pearl-kissed branch, pine
needles poking out of white hills, and
under those piled snowflakes, seeds
preparing for spring. *Patience,*
say the seeds. *Let the underworld
do its work while the city rests.*

INSIGHTS

The Knight of Pentacles reversed asks action-oriented minds to slow down, be patient, and let go of rigid expectations. The past is done and over with, the future unknowable. But the present—that's where we do our best work. This is a grounding card, reminding us that sometimes action is in the stillness. Like that Willie Nelson song goes, "Still is still moving to me." Our deepest growth and forward movement are in being still, turning inward, and tending the soul.

Despite being an introvert, I tend to be a pretty action-oriented person, like the knight in this card. This can make it hard for me to slow down and take pleasure in the journey rather than the destination. That's why I've had to develop such a strong self-care system! It's taken me a long time to understand the importance of everyday magic and learning to stay connected to it is an ongoing process. This card invites us to sink into that process and know that even when it seems like we aren't making progress, we are. Like the brown earth in the background of this card, we aren't barren, just holding seeds that will inevitably sprout and find their way to the sky. The most significant growth and most meaningful revelations come when we embrace the almost imperceptible changes within ourselves. That's when the healing happens.

THE FIVE OF CUPS UPRIGHT

I've forgotten to look for the golden
cups filled with sunshine
and the sturdy bridge
that will carry me home. The
water beneath it sweeps
away my sorrows and tattered
doubts that spilled from the fallen
goblets before me, once so heavy
with grief and things best left
in the past. It was a good thing the wind
knocked them down. I hadn't realized
how much they carried in their hollow
bodies. I don't need regrets, just hope.

INSIGHTS

The Five of Cups is up to the old mischief of the fives, presenting seemingly negative things that have genuine positive aspects underneath it all. These are gritty cards, shaking you up so you can see things more clearly. So, what is this card asking us to see when it walks into our lives? That we have abundance and possibility—if we stop focusing on the negative. In the card, a figure grieves over the loss of three overturned cups, oblivious to the two upright cups behind him, and the bridge that will lead him to a cozy home.

When we get tired and overworked, life can look bleak. When stuff happens to shake us up, we can forget all the beauty around us. This card asks us to recognize that while we may have gone through something distressing and need to process it, we also need to move on and see that we have two upright cups and a cozy home to find sanctuary in. The image literally tells us that the past is "water under the bridge" via the same image in the background of the card. Let go of what you can't fix and look toward the abundance right within your grasp.

THE LOVERS UPRIGHT

Here I am, naked except for the sun's rays kissing
neck, limbs, torso, face. I don't have the energy
to hide anymore. So here I am, hoping you
will join me. Let's dance and learn the song
of each other. The song of us. The song of sunlight
seeping onto our skin, burning away
the doubts and the fears and the
I'm-not-good-enoughs until all that's left
is the honey we make together.
Golden. Warm. Infinite.

INSIGHTS

Ahhh... The Lovers. What a delicious card to usher in the Winter Solstice and end the year! But it's not all kisses and flowers with this card, despite its amorous appearance. Like any reader of romance novels knows, the road to Happily Ever After is always a little bumpy and not without struggle. Why? Because love is about making choices and listening to your internal voice, a voice that, quite frankly, seldom falls in line with what mainstream society says will make you happy. Think about the stereotypical love triangle... There's the one that looks right on paper, and there's the one that's right for you. Sooner or later, you have to decide if you want to be "good on paper" or happy in life/bed/love.

And like any romance reader worth their salt understands, love isn't just about romantic love but also about loving yourself. In fact, in the best stories, the romance is almost always a by-product of a protagonist coming into their own as a person and learning to love themselves for who they are. So too with the Lovers card in the tarot. When this card walks into your life, it asks you to stay true to yourself and honor who you are. It means taking a hard look at the things that make you happy—and the things that don't. It's a unifying card, asking you to pull inward to achieve wholeness. It's got plenty of fiery passion too. There's no way you can cultivate healthy relationships with yourself and others if you don't bring a little heat into the mix. The Winter Solstice is the perfect time to do as the card asks: let the flames of your passion consume that which no longer serves you and nourish that which does. Be honest, be naked, be real about who you are and bask in the beauty of it!

THE EIGHT OF CUPS REVERSED

I have so many golden grails,
but the moon shines light on
what is missing. The sun tells me to ignore
the phantom chalice. To return to the world of brash
clanging cups. It's the moon I listen to. She
always knows what's best for me. Always
promises that I am capable of more than just my concrete-cup
accomplishments. I can be moonlight and unblemished
earth too. A story perpetually unfolding,
and the hope for something more.

INSIGHTS

I couldn't think of a lovelier card to start the new year with than the Eight of Cups reversed. It's an introspective card, reminiscent of the Hermit, asking us to reject the worldly pressures that take us outside of ourselves. Typically, the new year ushers in a rush of extroverted energy in the flurry of new year's resolutions to do, be, and have *more of* or *better*. Don't get me wrong, I love a good new year's resolution as much as the next person. The issue arises when resolutions stem not from better understanding and nourishing ourselves, but in asking ourselves to be something we are not. Examples abound: We don't just want to commit to a better fitness routine, but suddenly have the build of an Olympic gold medalist in four easy weeks, regardless of whether that is healthy or achievable for us. We want to give up sugar completely and never ever touch a glass of wine again instead of just getting more conscious about healthy eating habits. In that light, resolutions can seem pretty silly! I mean, what standard are we holding ourselves to?

Of course, this dynamic has more serious examples too, like overcommitting and overworking because you don't want people to think you're a big jerk-face when you say "no." But aren't healthy boundaries a good thing? For everyone involved? That's where this card comes in. It asks you to get quiet, get real, and get healing. In the image, there are eight cups perfectly aligned and balanced on one another. But there is clearly a missing cup, for which the Hermit figure goes in search. This represents the sense that something is off in your life or missing. The sun eclipsing the moon reflects the fact that you might have been caving to the demands of the extroverted world (the sun) instead of listening to your instincts (the moon—who knows all, including the emotions we don't think we should feel). If you don't listen to those feelings, they come out and make you feel like a LUNA-tic (see what I did there?). Suppressing your inner needs is a surefire way to make you feel crazy. Listen to the moon and your instincts. They will guide you back to yourself and your innate sense of well-being.

THE HANGED MAN UPRIGHT

Hold me tight. Wrap your burly branches around
me so that I may feel safe so suspended. So
that I may gaze upon the world with dizzy
eyes and feel my blood dance through
once listless limbs. Never have I known
weightlessness. Did the moon always shine
so when my feet were planted in the earth?
Did the songbird whisper such secrets? Did
your leaves always hold green spells of my
becoming? Did I always have these wings?

INSIGHTS

The Hanged Man. Like the Death card, this card is often misinterpreted as something negative or scary. In reality, these cards are about how terrifying it can be to change even though change is necessary for growth. We are in a perpetual state of becoming—ain't it grand?

The Hanged Man is all about getting a new perspective of the world. This is a card of surrender. Stop fighting the change. Pause. Take a breath. Feel what you need to feel, and, in the process, allow yourself to let go of what no longer serves you. This card typically walks into your life when you are feeling stagnant or stuck (and sometimes don't even know it!).

This is a tricky card, asking you to look for blessings in disguise and devils hiding behind angel faces, in short, shaking up how you've come to view your life. The only way you can do that is by taking a time out. Embrace this pause or the Universe will make you pause (seriously—ever pushed past the feeling that you need to slow down and then you find yourself sick and so forced to rest? That's the Universe taking matters into its own hands). Hang upside down suspended from the Tree of Wisdom. Let the blood rush to your head. Resist action in favor of contemplation. Enjoy the view. Let the answers come.

THE PAGE OF SWORDS UPRIGHT

There's so much to experience, but only so much time to lick and kiss and savor. So you must choose your devotions. Your curiosity must be your guide. Your hunger, the thing that makes you fearless. You are eager to be this passionate novice. The answers will come in time—with luscious, dedicated practice. In fact, you like not knowing—and so lay down your sword. Yield to the pull of pleasure. Flow. Taste. Tickle. Touch. Melt. Surrender.

INSIGHTS

Have you ever had so much energy you don't quite know what to do with yourself? Or you're brimming with ideas but haven't quite gotten around to committing to your next creative project? If so, you'd sound a lot like the Page of Swords, who is bursting with passion, inspiration, and enthusiasm... if only he could focus!

This card is about following that passion, welcoming joy into your life and doing more of what makes you feel whole. This is also an exploratory card—see how he is poised, ready for adventure? This card asks you to act on that energy and use it to explore what is right for you and your life.

The Page of Swords might be a novice, but he's a quick study and eager to learn, and as a result, always able to get to the bottom of things. But be warned, the card also reminds you not to get defensive as you go about your adventuring. You don't need to have your sword always at the ready for imaginary foes. It's better to be a happy rookie, unashamed of what you don't know but can easily learn with an open heart and mind. Remember what it was like to be an enthusiastic student? A passionate amateur? The great thing about this card is that it doesn't want you to be an expert; it just wants you to be open, more curious about the world around you and, in turn, eager to invite the good vibes in.

THE KING OF WANDS REVERSED

I have a scar that cut its way through
my knuckles and another lashed
across my forearm. Those are the ones you
can see. The others—and there are many—map
my journey back to myself. I've earned them all, loved
them all. They are my good luck charms. Ugly, gnarled
things that only need my fingertips across their puckered
landscape to reveal that I'm no novice, though
I find myself on the cusp of a new beginning.

INSIGHTS

Sometimes, it doesn't matter how successful we are, how accomplished, or how happy. Impostor syndrome inevitably rears its head, usually when we least expect it. One minute, we're living the dream, completely at home in our own skin and one with the Universe. The next... old doubts resurface, making us afraid to take the next step in our life. That's where the King of Wands reversed comes in. This is one tough dude, who's won his crown the hard way, using his survival skills to climb his way through the ranks. He's a reminder to stay strong, stay resilient, and stay positive.

Remember when I said self-doubt can pop up out of nowhere? Well, in reality, it usually appears when we are ready for the next step, moving outside our comfort zone, or taking a leap into the unknown. We become afraid, uncertain. We wonder if we have it in us to tackle this new obstacle, adventure, or opportunity. We worry that all our accomplishments are too good to be true, that we can't possibly conjure more abundance.

The King of Wands reversed reminds us to get with it! Being open to change and personal transformation is one of our strengths that have enabled our success so far. We can handle this next step too—like a boss or a king in this instance. All we have to do is believe in ourselves. That'll kill the self-doubt and open our energies to positive change.

THE TWO OF WANDS UPRIGHT

I stand inside my Eden because I once
dared to dream seeds would take root and
thrive in earth that seemed barren
to those who didn't know how to read
the soil. I have a home—a paradise really—
tucked behind four walls that holds
every celestial joy I could fathom. The world
in my palm—another handful of soil—asks me
to keep dreaming, to keep sowing seeds. Growth
is in imagining what can bloom if fed.

INSIGHTS

To a pessimist, The Two of Wands might conjure up phrases like "the grass is always greener," as the figure is looking out from his glorious estate toward the ocean, eager to experience more. The Two of Wands is a card of restlessness, stagnation, or, simply put, feeling like something is missing, but you can't quite figure out what. Have no fear, though, because this is not a card for pessimists—none of the cards in the tarot really are. The tarot is inherently hopeful, giving you insight that will help you better work in union with the world around you.

So, with that in mind, what does this card ask of you? To plan, to explore, to get ready for a new adventure. It doesn't mean to dismiss or devalue all that has come before, nor the abundance you currently enjoy. It simply gives you permission to keep growing, keep evolving. And, boy, do you have a great foundation for doing so! Think about your long-term goals and the groundwork you've laid out for yourself. Then consider where you want to go next. This card invites you to explore what the new chapter of your story looks like before diving right in. Supreme success will follow.

THE TEN OF WANDS UPRIGHT

I've forgotten what the sky looks like. I see
only the next step, feel the weight of ten
wands pressing their knobby knuckles
into my back. Then the wind comes, dries
the sweat from my brow, encourages
me forward. It feels so good to submit
to its care. I don't even mind when it knocks
some wands loose, sending them tumbling down
the path. Why was I carrying them again? No
matter. I can see the sky now.

INSIGHTS

Confession time: I'm all about the hustle. Seriously! I like working—teaching and writing—as much as I love slowing down and sinking into life's simple pleasures. In fact, a good day's work is one of my sacred simple pleasures. Why? Because I know so much magic comes from just showing up each day to do what you need to do. When we think of magic, like self-care, we can think of quick fixes (scented candles) and easy remedies (happy affirmations) in order to cultivate a joyful life. In reality, it takes work. A lot of work. Sure, magic is real, but the Universe needs to know you're working before your dreams begin to take shape. Put another way: it's kind of like writing a book. Sounds super cool and exciting, but it ain't gonna happen unless you show up to your writing desk every day (okay, most days) and commit words to paper. It's that simple. And, yeah, that hard.

The Ten of Wands is all about celebrating this energy. The end is in sight—you've got a nice home in the distance welcoming you and asking you to lay down your burdens. Woohoo! All your hard work has paid off, and you're about to reap your rewards.

This is a great time to reevaluate all the work you've been doing—and what's really worth your time. The Ten of Wands reminds you to take time for self-care and relaxation as you venture into an exciting new opportunity or take on more responsibility birthed out of your success.

It also asks you to shed any burdens you might have been unconsciously carrying. Have you been overworking to compensate for people not holding their own? Have you been drowning in unacknowledged emotional labor? Just because you can take on more work doesn't mean you should. Ask yourself, what is yours to do? Do that and let go of the rest.

THE ACE OF SWORDS REVERSED

I carry—protect—this *thing* with me. It's small
and fragile and held together by a few wisps
that make it fly and a heavy seed at its base
that keeps it from running away. That's my one wish,
strong and light as a dandelion seed. That's the only
name I have for it now—*thing, wish*—I'm not even sure
what it's becoming. I just know it's mine. And I want
to see what it grows into.

INSIGHTS

I love spring. There's something about it that whispers new beginnings. The days are getting longer. Bulbs planted in the fall burst through the earth, an annual reminder of the joy that blossoms after a long winter of quietly tending yourself. Even the air feels perfumed with possibility.

That's the kind of energy the Ace of Swords reversed asks you to protect—a fresh start, a new way of being—like you would a seed not quite ready to be planted. There are times in our life for action, but this is not one of them. This card asks you to protect this emerging side of yourself and lightly, tenderly explore what it could become. You probably aren't ready to share it with anyone yet, and that's okay.

In fact, the Ace of Swords is asking you to keep this delicious secret to yourself for now. It's so new, so sweet that you don't want anyone or anything to mess with it until it's stronger, ready to take on the world. This card is about vulnerability, allowing yourself to care for a new soul-nourishing seedling, but also in moving from feeling disempowered to being empowered. Sometimes it is our very vulnerabilities that give us strength. So go forth into this spring, protecting the new person you are becoming and exploring who she might be.

THE QUEEN OF PENTACLES REVERSED

I am Queen. Sovereign of my kingdom stretching
from the center of my solar plexus toward
my garden gate. The finches know it. The bees too.
So do the radish seeds and dandelion heads. Together,
we make up quite the kingdom, with our paperback seeds
and thyme-laced stories. I hush the fretful bunny that urges
me to plant more lusty words and daffodil bulbs. It is enough. I am
enough. I'm allowed to watch my stories bloom.

INSIGHTS

What a delicious card to get for the Spring Equinox, the season of fertility, coming abundance, and all-around fresh inspiration. The Queen of Pentacles reversed features a royal figure sitting on her throne and enjoying the surrounding beautiful garden and wildlife—her kingdom. This card is all about honoring your Queen status. This card in reverse specifically wants you to honor the hard work it takes to rule a kingdom… and pull back a little. Sometimes you have to give yourself permission to care for yourself, to take that responsibility as seriously as you would the care of others. You do enough and you are enough.

It's also about trusting your powers—you are a Queen after all—a fully capable person who cultivated the beautiful garden you now sit before. Let go of fretting and worrying about what could be, like the anxious rabbit at the top of this reversed card. You can't control the future, and, in the meantime, you are ruining your present joy by trying to anticipate potential problems that might come your way. Forget all that—and stop looking for trouble when there is none to be found.

Instead, get used to tending your joy. Turn your attention inwards. Apply all your leadership skills and thoughtful care toward healing yourself. Pause, rest, enjoy your garden. The Queen of Pentacles reversed reminds us that our growth and prosperity are already in motion—our seeds will bear harvest, whether we fret over them or not.

THE KING OF PENTACLES REVERSED

I have so much to do. A host of weeds
to uproot and even more seeds
to lay down. A story to write—no,
several. Instead, I go
on a walk. I visit my herb store. I make
tasty things from those weeds—medicine, I see
now—and eventually find my way to my desk to tend
my literary garden one word, one seed
at a time. I'm no good at hard rules. I
flow. The magic follows.

INSIGHTS

I'm often asked about my writing process. Many authors have strict schedules and certain daily page or word counts they have to meet. More power to them, I say, but I've never been able to do that myself. My writing has always been a mercurial entity, not liking being tied down or forced into a certain schedule. Yet I'm highly productive, writing a little every day and always eager to hit the page running. Why? I stay loose, let the words speak to me, let the stories flow as they want to. I lose track of time in the kitchen or garden, get into mischief, and inevitably find my way back to my writing desk, full of life experience, to sink into my words. As a recovering academic, I can't get too severe about anything, least of all my writing, or my magic dries up.

This is the wisdom of the King of Pentacles reversed: stay loose, even as you know what you need to get done. Know the value of time, creativity, money, and energy. Don't give it away willy-nilly, but don't hoard it either. Practicality is all good and well, but you must leave room for the dreaming; otherwise, nothing gets done. See what I mean? You can't get too worked up or rigid about anything; just trust the energy of the day.

THE KING OF SWORDS REVERSED

I grew from a crack in the concrete many
said wasn't hospitable—I saw the open
invitation in the dirt spilling from broken
man-made things. I knew fertile soil when
I saw it, and a space that wouldn't ask me
to hide my medicine. If I demurred, it would coax
me into letting the sunlight tickle my
eyelids, mouth, nose. Here,
I wouldn't have to be a weed.
Here, I could bloom into infinite
wind-kissed wishes.

INSIGHTS

I'm drawn to the power of dandelions in this card as I see them spilling out of sidewalks, lawns, and garden beds. They are the true unsung magic of the plant world. They are relentless with their medicine, finding their homes in places most people would consider inhospitable. They keep coming back despite vigorous weed-whacking and pulling. And they are cheerful as they do so! Always turning their bright yellow faces to the sun in delight, and, when the time is right, transforming into wind-kissed wishes that will become more medicine that cleanses the body and spirit and makes room for hope.

Dandelion medicine is similar to the medicine of the King of Swords reversed. This card is all about embracing your quiet power, trusting in yourself, even when others want you to forget that you are magic. Not only are you magic, but you are secure enough that you don't need to draw attention to yourself or show off all the time. You know who you are, so let your work, your energy speak for itself. Think of yourself as the dandelion: those who want your medicine will find you. Those who don't? They will see only a weed—and it won't matter one bit, or at least it shouldn't! If it does feel like those projections would matter to you, the King of Swords reversed asks you to shed those self-limiting beliefs—like the ugly thought that you might be a weed instead of magic. Take heart, and dare to imagine that you have an infinite capacity of transformation and joy.

THE FOUR OF CUPS REVERSED

I have a universe inside me I retreat
into when my little corner of the world
gets too loud and my soul too tired
for small talk and small
minds. There are books and a garden
and my dearest friends—
constellations and characters—
plus, seeds and dreams and the parts
of me I sometimes forget to tend. There, I
drink chamomile tea and rub juniper
salve across my body. I fill my heart
with desert medicine and hope.

INSIGHTS

Sometimes it can feel like everyone is racing through life, addicted to busy-busy-busy, a feeling that can be magnified when spring invites restless spirits to get more active after the long winter indoors. When the Four of Cups reversed comes into your life, it's asking you to slow down and pull in. I find it infinitely synchronous that I pulled this card near the end of my teaching year, when I was still learning to make time for self-care in the midst of the frenzied energy of the last few weeks of the term.

This was a hard lesson to learn, and one I continue to understand the nuances of. In short, going full-speed all term, only to experience nothing short of shock at an open schedule once final grades are uploaded is a painful experience. The transition is too abrupt, and I found myself creating work when I should be taking time to rest and slow down simply because I didn't know how to just be. Yes, even someone who writes constantly about self-care is still learning softer, gentler ways of living!

This card helped me break my addiction to busy. Instead, I learned to take time for myself. I indulged in quiet time. I made lovely dinners. I did yoga. I lost track of time and relished my necessary introversion. I spent time with family. It is essential to shamelessly enjoy the radical self-care the Four of Cups reversed asks you to sink into. While you take your own time to rest and rejuvenate, let go of old doubts and limitations and get ready for new delicious adventures. Relinquish what weighs you down to leave room in your life for what truly nourishes you.

THE TWO OF PENTACLES UPRIGHT

There is so much to do. Another
book to write—and so many
stories, my fingers can't type fast
enough. Shelling fava beans
is what I find myself doing, though,
and chatting with the morning birds
about what a wet spring it has been.
Plus, there are tulips to tickle, some books
to finish reading, a violin that needs
stroking. No time for writing!
Yet the stories get written
all the same. Perhaps all the better
for these distractions.

INSIGHTS

Have you ever found yourself thinking something along the lines of "if only my life weren't so hectic or complicated, I'd finally be able to (fill in the blank)?" The Two of Pentacles is here to crush that limiting idea that we must always be productive, that the bumps and plot twists are distractions rather than meaningful additions to our lives.

This card is all about going with the flow and letting your attention drift to what calls to it. Some days, it's work; others, family time or that ever-unfinished to-do list. Sometimes it's even about taking a long nap or getting lost in a good book. The point is that we have to let go of the idea that we will be able to accomplish certain things when life calms down because, in all honesty, life is always complicated! And therein lies the joy, inspiration, and bliss of living. In fact, your passion projects will be all the better for being flavored by the various things you must tend to in your daily life.

THE THREE OF SWORDS REVERSED

Your heart has been reshaped
by three sorrows as sharp
and cold as steel blades. It will never
know smooth skin unblemished by purple,
gnarled scars or a time without phantom
aches when the world wears you down.
So, it must become like the roots of trees—
flexible, growing in and around hard things
so that you have a solid foundation to reach
for the light. Still pumping blood. Still
beating. Learning to savor
rays through tree branches.

INSIGHTS

Well, this is a tough one. Have you ever just felt like life has kicked the stuffing out of you? Or that it feels like you're trapped in a telenovela with one escalating drama after another? We all have those days, months, or years (yikes) where life can get pretty intense. The good news is that the Three of Swords reversed is a hopeful card, signaling the end of heartache. It won't be pretty, and it won't always feel good, but you'll be able to take comfort in no longer sugar-coating toxic situations, throwing in the towel, and letting go of things that just aren't working anymore.

This card, for all its violence and ugliness, is an optimistic card when reversed. It's about acknowledging the pain and allowing yourself to move on. This doesn't mean that you should walk right back into the situation that caused you all that grief, mind you, or enable toxic behavior. It simply means that you should give yourself the space to process the heartbreak—which may take time, since three swords through the heart is a lot to heal from! Then move forward into your own abundance and joy.

Heartbreak is an inevitable part of life, but what matters is how we deal with it. Do we keep exposing ourselves to people, places, situations that want us heartbroken? Or do we learn, heal, and allow ourselves to move on from the heartache? This card reversed reminds us not to hold that grief for too long, because it is too easy to stay stuck in the constellation of that heavy energy. Instead, look to what brings nourishment, joy, healing, and take heart (pun intended) in the space you create for possibility when you let go of the unhealthy situations that were sapping you of your happiness.

THE MOON UPRIGHT

Tonight, it is just me and you. I'm
not afraid to get naked and show
you everything—so long as you
do the same. Let me howl
at your beauty, and you can bathe
me in your luminous truth. I like teeth
marks and secrets—so long as both are yours,
so long as it is you whispering my name.
So long as we can dance under the stars. Let's forget
we're rational creatures and simply feel. Feast.

INSIGHTS

Nighttime. Full moons and howling wolves. The time when lovers meet under the cover of darkness and stars are the only witnesses to the stories half-hidden in shadows. None of us can escape the lure—and the fear—of darkness. Even though we are creatures of daylight, we are no strangers to things that go bump in the night. And it's best to remember that. So says The Moon. She asks us not to be afraid of the dark or the unknown. Instead, we should make our home in them, seek out the shadows, and talk with The Moon. We are, after all, wild creatures ruled by the waxing and waning of the moon, however rational we try to be.

When this card appears, it's a good idea to think about how your feelings and instincts are shaping your present reality. The Moon has no light of her own, remember, but glows from the sun's light reflected onto her. This suggests that our inner workings—thoughts and feelings, conscious or unconscious, shape how we see things. This card asks us to examine unconscious habits or old ideas about ourselves that no longer serve us, and get rid of them so we don't let them taint our view of the world.

The Moon also represents intense female energy. Traditionally, this is a card about fear and the scary things the light of the moon can illuminate. But that's old school toxic patriarchy for you—always afraid of what it doesn't understand. In that limited ideology, the dark is evil, the unknown is evil, and the sacred feminine is suspect. This card asks you to push back against toxic patriarchy that limits all genders. Instead, this card wants you to sink into this quiet, wild feminine energy. Don't be afraid of the dark or the unknown. Instead, ask The Moon to guide you. What is it that she is asking you to see?

THE EIGHT OF PENTACLES REVERSED

Here I am, pounding pentacles
into silver coins as flexible
and light as fish scales. Day
after day. I make as many as I can until
my fingers hurt and my eyes
can no longer make out the starry
outline of my magic. That's the price you
have to pay to craft fins and scales
strong enough to withstand
the ocean waves' insistent kisses
and light enough to let you glide down
into the watery depths of imagination.

INSIGHTS

I love the sound of bees zooming around, tirelessly pollinating each plant they harvest from. I hear them each morning when I take my daily walk around the neighborhood and each afternoon when the flowers in my garden are fat and inviting, ever eager for the bees' touch. They are much like the Eight of Pentacles, a card that, when upright, is all about buckling down and getting work done. It's about honoring your calling and acknowledging the hard work it takes to develop it.

The Eight of Pentacles reversed, however, walks into your life when you are either resisting the hard work you need to do or, as was my case at the time, needing to embrace the ebb and flow of the elusive work-life balance. Yeah, okay, so I sometimes can be prone to overwork, but that's because I love what I do. I get caught up in the inspiration of the day, high on diving into a new project, excited about reaching the finish line. I'm learning to pace myself and create space for the energy to flow. Rather than getting locked into a rigid expectation of what my work life should look like, I'm learning to listen to my inspiration and creativity so that my work is a fluid exercise. Strangely, I'm more productive—and refreshed—this way!

The Eight of Pentacles reversed doesn't want you to give up that vital energy, only temper it and see that rest and relaxation are a vital part of your creative, productive life. This card also asks you to examine the kind of energy you're bringing to your work. Are you bringing positive, regenerative energy to what you do? Or are you weighing yourself down with negativity and stressing over what might be? Your intentions toward your work are important. Good vibes can make a seemingly mundane task invigorating because it helps you complete the overall picture; bad vibes can weigh down even the most exciting project. Part of honoring your calling, in my case as a teacher and writer, is making these things integral, seamless parts of your life, but not your whole life. See the difference?

THE SIX OF PENTACLES UPRIGHT

I'm both beggar and banker. Gold
flows through my veins, and I'm
half-ashamed of the way it makes
my bronze skin glow. I'm uncomfortable
with the sun's kisses—the unbearable
pleasure rippling through me is surely a sin.
So I give them away—my penance—
until I realize I don't have to be an empty
vessel. I'm allowed to be whole. I push
every last ounce of light into
my broken pieces and make it so.

INSIGHTS

Wow! Lots of pentacle energy these past few weeks. The pentacles, or coins in some decks, are all about security—emotional, financial, the works. They are associated with the earth, and so the basic things we need in order to thrive. Enter the Six of Pentacles, which depicts a wealthy figure bestowing coins to the poor. This card is all about generosity of spirit. If you need help, the Universe has your back; if you've got more than enough, you're able to give back. But this is the tarot, after all, so we need to get a little more poetic than that. Money is always symbolic of energy, the metaphysical currency that enables us to heal, grow, change—or, if we've depleted our reserves, stay stuck and stagnant.

Lately, I've been marinating on the ways in which we can be stingy with ourselves, even though we have the power and resources to heal ourselves and welcome light into our lives. Real talk, if you're a mestiza bruja with even a passing exposure to Catholicism, you might find yourself perpetually guilty for your abundance and so, find little unconscious ways to make yourself suffer. Traditional religion instills much shame in joy. So we get stingy with ourselves, we only allow ourselves so much happiness, and we hold back from our fullest expression of self.

To me, the Six of Pentacles is about gratitude for what we've accomplished and allowing ourselves to feel the full power of that. To shamelessly celebrate the healing and magic our hard work has wrought. This accomplishment could be spiritual, personal, or creative, not just monetary (although, true to cosmic law, you get your metaphysical stuff together, and your outer life becomes more abundant as a consequence). In essence, we are all both bankers and beggars. The magic is in channeling our energetic riches to bring healing to the parts of ourselves that are starving and in need of love. We deserve to thrive.

THE KING OF CUPS UPRIGHT

I have a sea inside me that storms
and dances—even I don't know
the full breadth and depth of it. I just catch
glimmers of it here and there when the waves
lap against my ribcage or the sunlight glitters
off its mirrored surface. I am a bottomless
mystery—to myself especially—yet my
sturdy sea legs navigate each swell
and dip, grounding me to the earth
as I let the cleansing salt water rush over me.

INSIGHTS

Here is a lovely card. The King of Cups is all about love and feelings. The King is more of a poet, able to navigate the sea of emotions we often find ourselves adrift in, and, like any good ruler, he wants what's best for his people. He's compassionate, happiest when he and those around him are flourishing. He is one of the many great examples in the tarot of healthy masculinity.

Notice how he sits above the sea rather than being swallowed by the waves. He feels deeply, understands deeply, but does not allow himself to drown in the ebb and flow of intense emotions. He is like the ship in the background of the card: able to navigate the mysteries of the deep seas without drowning because he has solid boundaries that prevents the water from overtaking him.

The King of Cups is asking you to find peace, even in the face of difficult emotions. He wants you to be compassionate and know the depths of your feelings. But he also wants you to consider which fears and joys you chose to feed: Your feelings become your reality, so choose the ones that fill your life with joy.

THE SIX OF WANDS UPRIGHT

I make my own magic.
That's how I got here—with the laurels
and the dancing and the parade. But
I'm not here to sit on the back of white horses
or gaze upon the crowd to see who celebrates with me—
and who sends me ugly thoughts. I merely did
what I needed to. What was in me
to do. And I continue to, casting the next intention
so that it may burst from its seed—alive.

INSIGHTS

The wands are all about fire energy, so there's no use playing coy or demurring when they enter your life. Take the Six of Wands; it wants you to celebrate! This card is all about enjoying well-earned accomplishments and recognition. This isn't about gloating, mind you, but about owning your magic and the hard work that's gone into achieving your goals.

The people who support and love you couldn't be happier for you, but there's always one (or several) in the crowd who is envious of your proverbial victory parade, as evidenced by the scowling face in the backdrop of the card. Guess what? Haters gonna hate. There's nothing you can do about it, so this card asks you not to waste time or energy on any negative vibes sent your way. Be unapologetic about who you are, and embrace your own personal brand of magic. It got you this far, after all. There's still plenty of work to do—this card is a six, not a ten, which completes the cycle of the minor arcana—but this card invites you to embrace the next adventure, just as soon as you finish partying. But before you go full-steam ahead, enjoy all you've earned and take this time to relax and reevaluate your priorities so that your next step is as prolific as the last.

THE HIEROPHANT REVERSED

I kneel before no one. I will not
open my mouth for blood and bread—
I have plenty of both. I will not pray
for answers or redemption. I refuse
to look outside myself for answers written
so plainly on the inside of my skin, truths
I'm still learning to voice fluently. Instead, I
will speak directly to the stars.
They know I'm barely contained divinity.
They don't force me to kneel,
only offer light to write by.

INSIGHTS

They say looking for love in all the wrong places can be applied to enlightenment too. We take classes, we read books, and we are forever in search of the next guru or religion to offer us comfort and advice. All good and well—heck, I've done plenty of all those things and found great wisdom and healing in them. Well, except the religion part, since mainstream religion is something that has been more oppressive than fruitful to me as someone with the violence of colonization written in her blood. As a result, my reading of the Hierophant, typically symbolizing a religious leader like a priest, is on the bruja side, which is always questioning the authority of mainstream figureheads, religious or otherwise, especially those that want us to proverbially bend the knee.

The trouble comes when we think these things are more magical than we are. We literally disempower ourselves by looking for cosmic answers or epiphanies outside of ourselves, especially when we are forever looking to a guru, saint, god, or other seemingly divine being to lead the way. Guess what? We can be pretty darn divine too.

Enter the Hierophant reversed. This card is all about honoring your rebel heart and rejecting the social norms that ask you to give up your sense of self for the sake of the status quo. It asks you to reject anything that starts with, "That's how things have always been done." Instead, embrace the wonderful, weird, wild life you've carved out for yourself simply by daring to trust your inner compass.

THE TEN OF CUPS UPRIGHT

My home is a four-chambered heart.
Too few rooms, some say. Only
so many people can fit in them. But
this beating thing holds as much
as it needs to. As much as it can. Plenty
of room for sunlight, stories, and seeds
—lemon balm and hope—
but none for shadows or nosey
neighbors (a small miracle).
Take my kitchen table, overflowing
with teapot, ceramic mugs, and
chamomile-laced conversations. Truly,
what more does a woman need?

INSIGHTS

The Ten of Cups is all about gratitude. Appreciation of what you have and what you've conjured from your own blood, sweat, and tears. It takes constant conscious conjuring to welcome health and good vibes into your home and banish the life-diminishing and toxic. With that focus and a whole lot of love, life is pretty darn good.

This card asks you to step back to see clearly the bounty of your life—in love, family, hearth, and home—and embrace the joy of it all. This isn't about perfection or a bump-less road. It's about knowing that you've built a home that can handle the inevitable bumps and bruises that come your way.

There's also a bit of trickster energy to this card as it reminds you that the reason you feel this closeness with loved ones and fullness of life is because you've chosen your own path and trusted your instincts. If you've been doubting yourself or your vision, this wonderful card tells you to keep creating space for things that nourish you and your vision. Forget the path others expect you to take—going your own way has brought you all this magic, after all. And that's no small thing.

THE THREE OF PENTACLES REVERSED

I was not made to collect
grains of sand—I am
not an hourglass (my figure
is proof enough of that).
In fact, I don't even need
to count hours or hold
the infinite seconds
that make them up at the base
of my spine. Mine is a body
meant for dance, exploration, possibility.
How much you can see—taste—
accomplish when you allow yourself to be
more than someone else's timepiece.
I'd rather be an unending song.

INSIGHTS

The Three of Pentacles reversed got me thinking of the *Phantom Tollbooth*. Truth be told, I don't remember much about this story from my childhood, except for a warm, fuzzy feeling. But one particular moment has stayed with me all these years. In it—at least according to my faded memory—Milo is asked by a seemingly nice, faceless man to move a pile of sand one grain at a time. Milo begins to feel that this is a pointless and time-consuming activity, and, once he realizes how long it will take to complete his task, decides to leave. During his escape, he finds that the kindhearted man he was trying to help was really the demon of petty tasks and worthless jobs.

There's a whole lot I'm leaving out of the story, but the part that is relevant to this card is that Milo had to give himself permission to move on from those grains of sand. No one else could do it for him—not his friends, certainly not the demon, or any other "helpful" soul. He had to decide for himself that what he was doing was not worth his time or energy. He had other adventures to embark on.

Such is the wisdom of the Three of Pentacles reversed, which asks you to examine your workload. Are you working smarter and not harder? Are you putting in more time and energy into a project than it merits? Whatever the case, pull back, reframe your priorities, and balance the scale. This will help you open up your energy, so the work you do is fluid, joyful, and purposeful, rather than doled out by the demon of petty tasks. Sooner or later, you have to give yourself permission to move on. To do less.

To free yourself from mindless busy. You're the only one that can.

THE QUEEN OF SWORDS REVERSED

She gifts me an apple. I take
the offering—it's impolite not to.
And we're taught to be ashamed
of being thought impolite. It's a luscious,
edible ruby in the palm of my hand.
Tempting. Nourishing. Everything
I need—if I didn't know something's wrong
with it. Poison in the flesh. There'll be no
bringing it to my lips. She has magic, true—
but so do I. I'm not afraid
to turn away rotten fruit.
Politeness be damned.

INSIGHTS

The Queen of Swords reversed represents the energy best known for conjuring evil queens, black widows, and other unsavory dark feminine energy. (These, to be clear, are different from the Dark Goddess, which can be a very powerful and positive archetype. Dark doesn't always mean bad. Just sayin'.) All that is loving and nurturing mother energy becomes cold and destructive under the stewardship of the Queen of Swords reversed. Instead of fostering encouragement and love, they plant seeds of self-doubt, isolation, and destruction.

But, as with all tarot cards, even the negative ones, there is hope. It's reminding you to trust your instincts and stay away from negative people—those evil queens and black widows. You know the kind: the ones who leave you feeling bad about yourself even though, technically, the meet-up was pleasant, or the situation that seems just fine but gives you a bad taste in your mouth. That's the problem with the evil queen in Snow White, for example—she puts up a good front as a well-meaning apple seller, caring ruler, and a myriad of other seemingly harmless personas. You have to peer behind the glamour to see the badness underneath.

This is also a card about knowing your truth—no matter how unglamorous or untidy it can feel to speak it. Don't be afraid to rock the boat. Suppressing your instincts and needs to appease some outer force never works well for anyone. So, shake off the evil queens of the world and remember that you are sovereign over yourself!

THE PAGE OF CUPS UPRIGHT

I hold a golden cup in my hand.
Within it is a universe with the mouth
of a fish. It whispers its secrets to me.
I must only listen deeply and hold
space for this conversation made of fish scales
and stardust. In time, I will understand the words
and knowledge swirling in this bottomless cup. I will
become the fish and the liquid cosmos
cupped in my hand. For now, I need
only open myself to possibility.

INSIGHTS

This card speaks of openness. Curiosity. Creativity. The importance of being receptive to the joyful wonders of the world and our own capacity for growth unfettered by expectations or experiences. It's the Page of Cups, after all. Pages are all about new beginnings, flirtatious energy, and the buoyant and fruitful curiosity of childhood. It's not action-oriented like the knight or complete like the Empress or Priestess. Instead, it speaks of receptivity, unfolding, of asking the Universe to speak to you, and being open to the answers it whispers in your ear.

I originally drew this card before heading out to a contemplative practices retreat, my first professional conference outside of my state in some time. I wasn't sure what to expect, and when I drew this card before going, I held off from writing my Tarot Tuesday story until after my time with The Center for Contemplative Mind in Society, since the card was clearly telling me not to be forward-moving, but to allow myself a period of space and openness to explore, learn, and nourish myself.

As it turned out, the summer session ended up being a deeply nourishing retreat both personally and professionally, and it freed me up enough to make some important changes for a more balanced, magical life. When The Page of Cups enters your life, look for love—self-love, love of community, maybe even romantic love—in unexpected places.

THE QUEEN OF CUPS REVERSED

There's plenty to do. So many hungry
mouths begging for nourishment. You lock
the door to your home instead. You make pillowy gnocchi
kissed by garden basil and sun-gold tomatoes.
Just for yourself, as the record player teases
out Billie Holiday songs. It's your belly
that needs attention. Your soul that needs
to remember what fresh garlic tastes like.
And when the cat chews through
an electrical cord—well,
that's just an excuse to go off the grid.

INSIGHTS

I pulled this card after a series of complications. My internet went out. My computer needed a check-up. My home demanded my full attention as I Marie Kondo'd and cat-proofed it, having met and adopted my familiar a few short weeks before. Oh, and I learned how to make eggless pasta. You see where I'm going with this? I should have been upset by the first few items I listed—they seemed to make my life more difficult, after all—but I wasn't. In fact, the time I had unplugged from the realm of technology allowed me to pull inward and recharge my batteries (even as my laptop battery was being replaced). The time cleansing my home of old energies and old selves served as a healing mediation on years of growth and transformation that had brought me far—and where I still need to create space for more growth and more healing. The Queen of Cups reversed spoke to me of turning inward and focusing on hearth and home. It was exactly what I needed, especially before starting a new teaching year.

This card asks you to slow down and absorb the wonder and abundance of your life. You might be accomplishing quite a bit, but this card asks that you don't just move from one project to the next without fully absorbing all you have dreamed into fruition. Life is about the little moments you take to feel what you need to feel and enjoy the life you have created for yourself. This queen is all about nourishment of the self—with a touch of caution thrown in, as you might be one of those souls that gives out a lot and forgets to take care of yourself when others demand your energy and attention. Hold space for those you're meant to, but remember not to carry their burdens—they have their own journey toward healing, as you have yours. So unplug, unwind. Put on an old record. Pour a glass of wine. Make yourself a beautiful homemade pasta dinner. Wellness starts in the kitchen, after all.

THE NINE OF SWORDS REVERSED

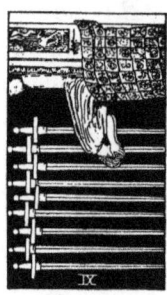

The shadows smother
you like a heavy blanket.
But you don't dare close
your eyes. That's when the thing under
the bed comes for you. There's only
one thing to do. You turn on the light.
Throw off your covers. And crawl
under the bed. The thing of horns, shadows,
claws, and fears whispers nightmares in your ear.
But they aren't so scary when you face
them head-on. You talk. You
feel better. You both sleep soundly.

INSIGHTS

The Nine of Swords is all about the nightmare state—all your complexes are fully activated, and your inner demons have come out to play. You just can't quite see them (the figure is covering their eyes) or the solution to banishing bad vibes and returning to the world of wonder and hope with eyes open. This is another one of those seemingly negative cards in the tarot deck because it's so charged. That said, I think the silver lining here is that it makes us aware of the things that go bump in the night so that we can open our eyes and face what we need to face. Like nightmares, these "bad" cards serve to illuminate what we can't always see in the light of day. They pop it out—the stuff we're afraid to see or our dark side—so we can't hide from it anymore.

But with the Nine of Swords reversed, you have a different kind of psychic charge. This card walks into your life when you've faced the nightmare, the old complex that has flared up, your inner demons. You've worked through it, recognizing the following: You are too hard on yourself, which can lead to self-doubt and negative self-talk. You can feed bad thoughts because of your impostor syndrome. Your inner saboteur can come out when you're around toxic people and negative situations. You can punish yourself for successes you don't think you deserve (a side effect of early childhood exposure to Catholicism, perhaps? That last bit might just be me).

Here's how you heal yourself: You have a heart-to-heart with the monster under the bed and listen to the scary things it wants you to face. You choose healing. You choose joy. You tune in to the wonder of the Universe. You celebrate yourself.

THE WHEEL OF FORTUNE UPRIGHT

I've asked too much of myself. Forcing
time and forging narrow roads when I needed wild,
open spaces. All it gave me was a clockwork heart
ticking rapidly as if it could shape my future
with its turning gears. It's no use. Fortune
has her own way. Her wheel turns just as it always has:
at its own pace. With its own purpose. I must trust
this celestial wisdom—give up
mechanical solutions and be human once more.

INSIGHTS

This card came to me when I'd been letting go of a lot of things, especially those rooted in insecurity or old ways of being. Things I'd stopped fixating on included outmoded ideas of what my life should look like, what I should be doing on any given day, or why certain things didn't happen and why certain things did. Things I'd learned to embrace included more time to just be, listening to the energy of the day and going from there, and allowing my life to unfold as it would without pressure for a specific outcome or despair at a bump in the road. This new way of engaging with my life was a revelation. I enjoyed things more and was less stressed by the inevitable curve balls that came my way. I'd found my center, grounded in my core sense of self that remained unruffled by external plot twists and nourished by slow, soulful living.

Guess what? That's the wisdom of the Wheel of Fortune. This card tells you that you're on track. If things feel down, you'll soon find yourself on the upswing. Things going well? Don't get too worked up if life gets complicated. Find your center, your foundation of joy, even when your world seems topsy-turvy. Happiness isn't about controlling everything but understanding and embracing the fact that life is a series of ups and downs, unexpected twists and turns—like any good story. What matters is that you don't get swept up into the outside drama that takes us away from ourselves. Focus on what you can control—your reaction to things and how you choose to live—and enjoy the wild ride of life. Upright, this card is particularly positive. Luck, good vibes, and delicious new adventures are around the corner.

THE SIX OF SWORDS REVERSED

I've tried to stop time or at least slow
it down. Foolish, I know—but
the impulse wasn't completely conscious.
I'd just gotten used to two fists wrapped
around grains of sand as if to keep them from gliding
through the supple curves of an hourglass.
I'm not sure what my hands will feel like—
what they might hold—if I let the grit cutting
into my lifeline slip away. Perhaps
I don't need answers, only open hands.

INSIGHTS

In what had become a six-month or so journey of letting go of things that no longer served me, I pulled the Six of Swords reversed. This is an interesting card for its sheer subtlety. In it, a rower guides a mother and child through choppy waters to safety. Guess what? It's a metaphor! If this card has turned up in your reading, it's all about leaning into the choppy waters aka the discomfort that comes up when you are in the process of change. Especially reversed, this card is about finding the places in your life where you feel stuck or stagnant and pushing through those muddy waters (another metaphor) toward smooth sailing.

Here's where the subtlety comes in: Sometimes we get stuck without even realizing it. Sometimes this even happens as we are in the midst of transformation. We become disoriented and a little confused, longing for the comfort of the past we know so well, even though it is no longer healthy for us. We seek out this comfort because the changes we make can make the future feel so uncertain. But, as with all cards in the tarot, this one has a silver lining: There's a safe harbor up ahead. Just keep rowing.

THE NINE OF WANDS REVERSED

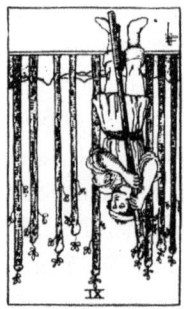

I walk home by candlelight.
Just beyond the blue flame, I
see flickers of things I
shouldn't look directly at. If
I tear my gaze from the road
before me, there's no telling
what kind of specters
will try to take me, what spirits
will seek to inhabit my body.
So, I focus on the hot kiss
of beeswax on my skin,
the way the moon holds me
close and the earth holds me
up. Home is within reach.

INSIGHTS

Have you ever been walking along, just minding your own business—having a marvelous time, in fact—when all of a sudden, you stumble into a Dead Zone? Cue creepy music and dark lighting reminiscent of a B movie. Suddenly, you're no longer happy. Every old ghost resurfaces and tries to possess you. Every complex is set off at once. The world becomes a study in gray and black, like something out of an old Twilight Zone episode. Nothing is what it seems. Welcome to the Dead Zone.

Dramatics aside, we've all been there. We take care of ourselves, we feel better, then we go someplace we shouldn't. That comes from the overconfidence that can set in when we begin to heal and welcome joy into our lives. We feel invincible—old things that hurt us, or negative situations seem less harmful under the rosy glow of our growth and self-confidence. But not so. In fact, we are so happy because we recognized those things weren't nourishing to us and moved on. It can be tempting, however, to try to reclaim things that went sour in the past and make them beautiful again—which is how we can find ourselves in the Dead Zone. We walk right back into the toxic stuff we needed to leave so long ago thinking—no, hoping—it wasn't really as bad as we remembered.

But never fear—we can always find our way out of the Dead Zone and back to happy and healthy. So says the Nine of Wands reversed. Appreciate your hard-won victories and the hard knocks that taught you a thing or two equally—then move on. Let go of the past, the ghosts, and anything else that would ask you to nurse resentments rather than the joy you've been cultivating so diligently. Focus on your own good energy and release the rest. Weave successes out of challenges and adventures out of stumbling blocks. And remember, there's no fixing Dead Zones, so best give them a wide berth. You've got plenty of joy to reclaim, which means you have no time for digging up old ghosts.

THE FOURS OF PENTACLES REVERSED

I willingly swallow the seeds
you offer. They are ruby gifts, ones I know
you painstakingly selected just for me. You
watch me as I let them slide down
my throat. When the last one finds my belly,
we hold each other close, eagerly
awaiting the stories that will sprout
from them and bloom between us.
There, in the darkness, we find ourselves
in hands stained from the pomegranate's broken
skin and the sticky aftermath of our storytelling.

INSIGHTS

Autumn is a season seemingly designed for introverts. We can shamelessly tuck into a good book at home as the days get shorter and the nights cooler. Curl under a cozy knit blanket and take a catnap on the couch—sometimes with an actual cat. And we can take long walks in the soft autumn afternoons, the whispering trees the loudest conversation around. It's the perfect season for the Four of Pentacles reversed, the card that asks you to reevaluate what's important to you—and to give yourself as much space, quiet, and time as you need to figure that out.

The pentacles are all about worldly comforts—money, accomplishments, the stuff you keep in your home, your home itself—all those things reflect the kind of life you want for yourself. You might be going through a decluttering phase, like I did that year, letting go of the things that no longer serve you. You might be unlearning lessons of mindless busy and overwork (also like me). You might be practicing the art of slow living and creating space for... nothing in particular. See where I'm going with this?

Sometimes we get loud, busy, ravenous in order to keep the silence, the stillness at bay. Because in the silence, in the stillness, we find answers. Answers that sometimes scare us. We have to confront feelings we haven't wanted to feel. We have to listen deeply to what our heart of hearts is telling us. And we have to let go of things that are holding us back—always painful, even when we know it is necessary. Never fear, however, because this card tells us that if we lean into the journey, catharsis and healing will find us. It wants us to be like Persephone, descending into the underworld each autumn. Don't be afraid. It's not death you'll find, nor hell. Think of the darkness as the promise of rebirth.

THE KNIGHT OF WANDS REVERSED

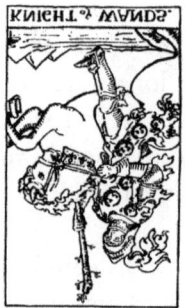

I resist the temptation to poke,
prod, stir. The fire that I've so tenderly
built up from dreams and twigs
is robust and burning on its own now.
The ingredients I've painstakingly harvested
from the earth and the underworld and the stars
are simmering in liquid imagination, carefully poured
from my mind into the cast-iron pot. The moon
holds first watch. I've done what I needed to. Everything
but rest. Now the magic must do its work.

INSIGHTS

I love it when I get a Stop and Rest card, and as life would have it, I was unable to write about it for about a week. It's really just what the cards wanted: for me to slow down, rest, and then return to writing after I've had time to process the wisdom the tarot offered me. This felt especially true after yet another reversed card that offered an interesting combination of the action-oriented (the knight) and the primal fire energy (the wands), both of which get turned on their heads with the Knight of Wands reversed.

Knights are about active energy, so you've got an aggressive combo with the fiery wands! Reversed, this card is all about appreciating the action in inaction. Real talk: this is hard for me. I'm a pretty action-oriented person. See a problem? Fix it! Feel inspiration… see where it goes! Need to conjure a little everyday magic? Keep working on it until you feel that spark ignite and grow into a robust flame. All good and well, but sometimes in the bluster and fuss of trying to get things done and find your place in the world, you can lose track of yourself. You forget to listen to the gentle whispers of the trees—they offer so much wisdom if you listen. Better to stop looking outside yourself and turn inward.

This card asks you to see the power of play, the action in inaction, the song in silence. Let the fire energy of the wands be a slow burn like you're letting something simmer on the stove all day until it is melt-in-your-mouth tender by dinner time. It doesn't always have to be fireworks and bonfires. The strongest fire is the internal flame you steadily tend so it won't go out. Let the knight's direction be turned inward. His quest might not be easily quantified like things in the external world, but it is all the more important for its mystery. Remain receptive to the mysteries of the self. It might not feel like you're doing anything—or that you're not doing enough. In reality, you're doing the most important work of all: self-discovery.

THE SEVEN OF SWORDS REVERSED

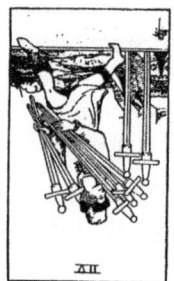

I ask rosemary to make me as strong
and brash as she is and lemon
balm to give me sunshine for rainy days. The earth—
so much I ask of her. To ground me. Hold me
as I see what I need to, then let me grow
roots deep into her heart, so I will never forget
myself. The wind whisks away illusions
and ugly thoughts. To her, they are nothing more than spectral
barnacles—useless for dreamers.

INSIGHTS

The Seven of Swords reversed marked the fifth week of reversals for me. It's a card that's all about seeing past what seems-to-be to what actually is. Clearly, the tarot was asking me to get a new perspective on things—looking at the world upside down rather than right side up, much like the wisdom in The Hanged Man, looking past illusions and understanding the truth of things.

Here's the tricky part: We struggle to know which is which. Here's the even trickier part: What the status quo decides is good, the mystic realm is decidedly against, most of the time. I've said it before, and I'll say it again, magic is a hard, gritty thing. It demands unadulterated honesty with yourself and what will truly be fulfilling and healing to you. You can't reach high and live low, ask for answers and refuse to listen, or dream deeply and disregard the spirit realm in your waking life.

If this card walks into your life, it's asking you to draw on your inner trickster and bypass the status quo. The impostor syndrome you've been feeling? Just another way to keep you from yourself. Get grounded. Listen to your instincts. Tune in to your inner life. Do that hard work, and you'll create your own luck. Rather, opportunities will arise as you trust yourself and your individual path. The magic always finds us when we've been working—on healing, on growing, on living.

THE SUN REVERSED

People try to give me rain clouds.
Not the fat, full life-bearing kind
that soak my seeds, coax them into blooming.
Theirs are swollen, sagging things that swallow
joy and never burst upon the earth
to nourish hope. Their dirty dishwater stories
don't belong to me and would only make my seeds
shrink back inside themselves. I'd rather have
sun—and the right kind of rain. Let them warm
my heart and give me puddles to dance in.

INSIGHTS

I often write about how much it takes to nourish our joy. It's a terrifying thing: joy. And sometimes we can feel guilty for having so much of it. But we have to remind ourselves how hard we've worked for those rays of sunshine.

That's the thing about bright, shiny feelings. People only see the sparkle—not the hard, hard work that goes into dealing with your shadows and planting seeds of hope. Joy can look effortless to those unaccustomed to tending that flame. So, we hold back from the sunshine and the right kind of rain so as not to draw attention to ourselves. The Sun card, however, tells us to let it shine, let it shine, let it shine. Even reversed, as it is here, it's considered the best card in the deck. When it walks into your life reversed, it's asking you to let your inner child out to play—and to avoid catering to cynics, nay-sayers, or run-of-the-mill downers. You've worked hard for your sunshine. Now enjoy it!

THE FOOL REVERSED

I can be so very foolish. The art
I make has more glitter
than talent stretched across
canvas. The gnocchi I lovingly roll out
—far from the edible pillows
of culinary fantasies. And my dancing!
It's hips, arms, and feet that don't
always go where they should. I read
tarot too, though I often
have to consult my books
to make sense of the two
by four inch cards. Yet
I still do all these things.
With relish.

INSIGHTS

There's an essay in my book, *Everyday Enchantments*, called "On Being an Amateur." It's about the pure joy of NOT being an Expert. You get to mess up. Make mistakes. Look ridiculous. Have fun—without needing to meet a certain standard. This is an energy I've tried to cultivate and celebrate in my non-teaching and non-writing self. I spent years after graduate school trying not to turn everything into a dissertation or master every new hobby I acquired. Instead, I gave myself permission to be just okay at something. Enthusiastically and wildly so-so. To experience that kind of hedonism, however, I've had to give up assumptions of how I think I should be doing things, let go of always being in control, and be at peace with making a fool of myself.

The Fool card in the tarot applauds those efforts! This card is all about seeing the world through the eyes of a child—full of wonder, curiosity, eager to experience this or that for no other reason than that it sounds fun. The Fool reversed—the card we have here—specifically asks you to shed any sense of self-consciousness about trying something new, release the fear of failure or rejection, and simply relish the possibilities and adventures life brings your way. It indicates you might be feeling blocked or unsure about your next step. You might even be getting stressed or uptight about the unknown. Impostor syndrome could be flaring up. So, the Fool reversed enters our reading to remind us to be playful. Literally! Bring more playfulness into your day-to-day life, no matter how small. Remember that the Universe has your back and applauds your willingness to be open to the magic of everyday life. Seek experiences outside of your comfort zone and find empowerment in being brave enough to call yourself an Amateur.

THE CHARIOT UPRIGHT

I draw strands of moonlight
and knit them into a semblance
of a blanket so that I
may always feel divinity wrapped
around my shoulders. Know the secrets
of the Universe whispered by stars
when the world gets too literal
and asks too much of me. I
don't want to be a so-and-so or know
a so-and-so or do such-and-such. In truth?
Quiet is a delicious thing.
I'm dizzy with the wanting.

INSIGHTS

My last card of the year had me leaving behind seven whole reversals and finding myself once again upright. There is no better card to be once again right side up than The Chariot. It is especially interesting to close out the year with a card that asks you to reevaluate who you are and to live your truth boldly.

There's a lot of fire energy in The Chariot. It's an assertive, masculine card pushing you to be strong and focused to achieve your goal. The figure in the card is a brave warrior promising victory if you keep your course. But this is the tarot, so there's always more than a little poetry to each reading. Being focused and fierce about what you want isn't just about the external world or the next gold star. It's about knowing who you are and what kind of life you want to live—then ferociously cultivating and protecting it. Being a warrior means a lot of different things and can manifest itself in different ways.

As I turned inward to celebrate this season of solitude and the gentle hush that only the Winter Solstice can bring, I found myself thinking about the courage it takes to live quietly, softly, in accord with the rhythms of nature, the unseen mystical world, and our own souls. The two sphinxes guiding the chariot in the card remind us that it is not through force or physical power that we move forward, but in releasing the reins (notice the figure holds none) and allowing the sphinxes to guide you deeper into yourself. It is something, in this loud, extroverted world, to nourish and protect our sanctuaries and the time we carve out for peace and quiet.

THE DEVIL REVERSED

I've forged chains from old selves. The weight
of those experiences is almost enough
to make me forget I'm part seed,
always able to thrive. This underworld
is merely the womb that warms my body
so that I may burst, bloom, and
once again return to life above ground.
There I will turn my heavy shackles into celestial
daisy chains. I'd once easily made things from nothing but starlight
and hope, after all. And I'd rather wear flowers.

INSIGHTS

Here's a great card to start the new year with: The Devil reversed, which depicts an escape from Hell. You know that old saying, "The devil made me do it..." This card asks you to flip that statement on its head, just as the card itself enjoys a reversal of energies. The loose chains around the figures can slide off easily in the reversed image, suggesting that it's not the devil keeping you trapped in your proverbial hell. It's all you. The devil's not making you do anything!

The good news is the old ghosts and demons holding you back aren't all that strong—the chains are easy to slip off—and you've done the work you need to free yourself from the terror of self-limiting beliefs and unhealthy fears and anxieties. All you have to do is let go. Easier said than done, but I'm drawn to the wisdom of the classic 80s movie *Labyrinth*. The way the heroine defeats the evil goblin king is by remembering and forcefully voicing that he has no power over her.

So when the thrill of the new-year-new-you fades and all your old self-doubts begin cropping up along with old toxic situations trying to draw you back in, repeat this mantra: *You have no power over me.*

Feel it. Know it. Own it. Take your power back.

THE FIVE OF WANDS REVERSED

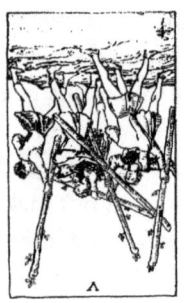

It is no small thing to learn
how to fold clothes in sync with the cumbia
playing in the background. Step back. Fold
shirt. Step forward. Place on bed
while your cat watches perched
on the pile of laundry warm
from the dryer. Wiggle those hips.
See what I mean? Hard to learn,
especially when you're used to battle
steps. Razor sharp focus. The next survival
strategy. Those I know. Laundry
cumbia? Maybe one day I'll master it.

INSIGHTS

The fives in the tarot fascinate me. They are the topsy-turvy cards where upright is chaos and reversed is returning to a sense of normalcy. Old-school tarot wisdom views the fives as negative cards, but I tend to think of them as healthy disrupters. They come in wild and crazy to shake us up and help us see what we need to see—just like the rest of the tarot, only with a heavier hand because we majorly need to get unstuck. They change the order of things and flip the script.

Add the passionate, fiery energy of the wands, and you have a card that asks to embrace this new order fully. The Five of Wands reversed asks you to take a deep breath after conflict (this could be internal or external—probably a little of both) and find your center. Use the fire energy of the wands to direct your energy to things that bring you joy. This isn't about avoiding conflict, but rather knowing how to redirect your energy to things beyond past struggles or restrictions. You know you can handle life's curveballs; now it's time to cultivate health and enjoyment. In fact, tending those things will help you build better boundaries. Get grounded, but don't be afraid of the trial-and-error process or the inevitable ups and downs. Simply sink into the process and new paths will open.

THE ACE OF CUPS UPRIGHT

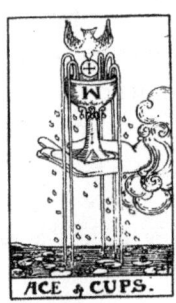

There's new life within my ribcage.
Like a hollyhock's bud bursting, spilling
its seeds across my chest. Each black disc
unfurls with a sigh, blissfully
no longer contained. Eager
to experience spring. Fresh green
tendrils poke in and around my ribs.
I am tempted to curl in on myself, protect
my tender belly from too-hungry hearts.
But these brash and budding flowers
will not let me be afraid.
They ask only that I let the light in.

INSIGHTS

Well, this is a delicious card. The Ace of Cups is an open invitation to welcome in love, joy, and all the juicy, glittery, bubbly, pleasurable energies of life. Like all aces, this card represents new beginnings, the first step in a journey. It's like a seed that you need to plant and care for if you want to see those lovely energies come to fruition. The cups are all about emotions and the psychic waters that flow through and shape our outer lives.

Sometimes, especially as we get older, we become more battle-hardened, with scars and scrapes proof of our missteps and heartbreaks. This isn't necessarily a bad thing. Experience, after all, makes us smarter (ideally, anyway). We can avoid the follies of youth and better understand ourselves, the world around us, and how to nourish healthy, meaningful relationships. Sometimes, however, we can consciously or unconsciously begin to hold ourselves back or perpetually keep our guard up in an effort to prevent more pain and scarring.

But here's the thing: We can be open to the good and still wear the armor that deflects the bad. Experience, in short, can teach us that we don't have to be all open or all closed, merely receptive to the goodness of life while honoring our hard-won life skills and knowledge that can keep us (more or less) away from the nonsense that drains our energy. The Ace of Cups asks you to do just that.

THE PAGE OF PENTACLES REVERSED

Remember who you are when the days
get long, and you feel buried under old scars. Remember
who you are when nights feel short, and you struggle
to feel the magic of the moon's silky kisses across your eyelids.
The wicked wind sweeps in, trying to take you
from yourself. Let it only take the dark tangles
clouding your mind. Remember, when you're tired of waiting,
that the Universe is always turning your wishes
into living, breathing things.

INSIGHTS

It was a dark and stormy day when I pulled this card, with the wind whipping through the city like some supernatural force in a gothic novel. Like any over-the-top natural phenomenon in these sorts of stories, it's meant to make the unseen worlds visible and literally whisk away stagnant energies and limited points of view that keep us from seeing the magical energies in and around us, guiding us to deeper ways of living... if we take the risk and listen to them.

The Page of Pentacles reversed is a lot like that dark and stormy day. It comes around when you are feeling stuck. You are trying every which way to take care of business or have a breakthrough. You can push and push, but all that does is make the energy more stuck. So stop trying so hard!

Instead, take pride in your hard-earned lessons and years of experience. Loosen the reins a little. You have the skills and experience necessary for whatever your task is, be it literal like finishing a big course design project (okay, super specific to my teacher life, no?) or something more intangible, like trying to be less work and more... unexpected magic.

It's easy to fall out of touch with your intuition and your inner self when you try too hard. Give yourself some space and time to recharge your batteries. The answers will come. Listen to what you feel like you are missing in your life and create space for it. Relax. Stop spinning your wheels and trust the Universe. Then let the wind sweep away all the tangled thoughts that you don't need.

THE NINE OF PENTACLES REVERSED

I sometimes forget I'm a seed
with an entire universe written
inside my shell. I'm allowed
to be infinite. But it's a funny thing
to allow. So many hungry mouths
want to swallow up that verb
so that I'm forever in search of permission
to bloom. I'm supposed to be a pebble
instead of barely contained cosmos.
But I won't allow it. Not for me. Not
for my stories. Not for the starlight
that illuminates my path.

INSIGHTS

It seemed the last third or so of the tarot deck was determined to upend the status quo with the many reversals it sent me. Gotta admit, I love it! The energy of reversed cards is the stuff of the mercurial trickster. It asks you to shed the shackles of mainstream such-and-such and follow your rebel heart—a scary thing when the rest of the world seems determined to fence you in. So strong is this pull to conformity that you begin to fence yourself in before anyone else can, one tiny inch at a time until you've forgotten what it's like to be expansive. The good news is that you have the power to take back those wild parts of yourself, even if you have to do it one inch at a time.

The Nine of Pentacles reversed tells you just how to do it. This card is all about reclaiming your sense of self-worth. Are there ways in which you've been taking yourself for granted? You may question your ability to energetically level up or attract the right kind of loving vibes into your life. You may struggle to stay out of lower-level thinking and relating. Or might be tolerating things that make you feel bad about yourself. Here's the thing: You are allowed abundance and joy in all parts of your life. This card gives you the cosmic permission you've been needing to take out the proverbial trash—toxic people, situations, thoughts, and old ways of being. Clean house. Get rid of anything that doesn't contribute to your higher frequency. Maintain your standards. Reap the rewards.

THE STAR UPRIGHT

I have the North Star inside of me.
It's a small steady light just under
my ribcage telling me where
I need to go. When the world feels dark
and my heart full of so many unspoken
worries and heartaches, this celestial core
bids me find my home in the garden
of possibility. I must plant my magic seeds
and dare to cast light upon
the parts of myself that have long
been dormant. I'm allowed to bloom.

INSIGHTS

Now here was a luminous, uplifting card during the week of the super full moon—and the last of the winter moons—along with Friday the 13th looming on the horizon (my favorite good luck day). It was also the card I drew at the start of the pandemic. COVID-19 had just come to New Mexico, and I was heading toward moving my classes online and preparing for a six-week lockdown, not to mention grappling with the fear and anxiety of all the unknown variables of keeping this deadly virus in check.

The Star might seem like a strange card to get with all that was going on in the world, but as always with the tarot, we must remember the poetry of a good reading. This card was like the healing balm of a cool spring breeze and the hopeful promise of better things to come—just what I needed amidst the panic of the early stage of the pandemic.

It's not about ignoring the difficulties surrounding you, but rather trusting your own resilience and life experience to see you through a difficult time. The Star is also out in the night sky, inviting you to get some emotional distance from your current situation and a big picture view of things (six weeks in lockdown is nothing, in the grand scheme of things, if it keeps people safe, for example).

In essence, it's a card reminding us to stay grounded but hopeful. On a more personal level, this card is about appreciating your sense of self and the hard work you've done to heal and make a home for yourself. Now is your time to replenish your inner well. See how the figure in the card waters dry earth? Give time and attention to the parts of yourself that have needed more nourishment. The seedlings are there, ready for your gardener's hand to coax them into manifesting. The Star, above all things, is a card that dares you to dream and aspire, so do so with abandon, knowing that each dream is a magic seed that will one day bear fruit.

THE TEN OF PENTACLES REVERSED

I let my feet become as tree roots
grounded in the earth while my body
bends and sways in the wind. I let the sun
comb tangles from my unruly
hair as birds whisper natural wisdom
in my ear. At night, the moon soothes me with her stories,
and the stars remind me that all things pass.
I am truly rich, to have so many wonders
to hold space for me and for me to love in return.

INSIGHTS

There are no two ways about it: It was a strange time out there as I continued on with my Tarot Tuesday project during the early days of the pandemic. But I took heart from the Ten of Pentacle reversed. This is a card of hope, particularly in relation to material things, as all pentacle cards are. When this card is pulled, it's about examining what is truly important in your life and celebrating what you have.

Avoid the impulse to accumulate unnecessary things or be a mindless consumer to feel a sense of security (seriously side-eyeing toilet paper hoarders as I wrote this). Instead, take a deep breath, know that you have enough, and that there is plenty to go around. You have a roof over your head (and many programs working to keep it so). Loved ones that are safe and sound. A whole community that cares about our individual and collective safety. And so many people willing to do their part, even if it is just practicing social distancing (a huge part in slowing the spread), to make sure that we all stay safe and well. That's what I call riches!

In a non-pandemic reading, this card asks you to get grounded and appreciate what you have. Stop reaching for more. Instead, celebrate your hearth and home, family and friends, and take time to think about what really matters. Have gratitude for the life you've created to combat scarcity mentality that creeps up when you're feeling insecure.

THE QUEEN OF WANDS UPRIGHT

Today, I'll take my cue from the sunflower
who never fails to turn her face
toward the light. This is why she has a strong
spine, fat mustard petals and thick seeds
to scatter across the earth. Today,
I will celebrate the quiet magic
things, like a black cat sitting
lazily on my windowsill. He, too, basks
in the sunlight. Today, I'll harvest joy
as if it were those black sunflower
seeds ready to burst, fat and full.

INSIGHTS

We got another hopeful card to get during the third week of social distancing in New Mexico. The Queen of Wands is all about hope, turning your face toward the sun, and remembering that magic is in the everyday. When she walks into your life, she's asking you to stay brave, bold, and, well, beautiful, if we're keeping this alliterative.

This queen is a bit of a social butterfly, asking us to relish our connection to others and, perhaps more importantly, our connection to self. It was so easy to become disconnected from self and others during that scary time. The Queen of Wands, however, said there's no need to feel isolated or adrift. Look to the light within. Just by practicing social distancing, we were doing so much good. Then look for light out in the world. There were so many people working to resolve this situation, from scientists finding cures and helping those that were sick, to artists, writers, and others helping their communities stay connected and supported at this time. See what I mean? So much love and compassion in the world!

In a general reading, she's asking you to go your own way and love every minute of the journey. She's social and kind-hearted, but she's not afraid to claim her independence or live life on her own terms. Here's my favorite part about the Queen of Wands: She LOVES black cats. She doesn't care that they have a lot of superstitious baggage tied to them. She simply knows that they are magic and celebrates them for it. This is the reminder that, once you've gotten your fill of light and time connecting with others, follow the black cat and retreat into the realm of the quiet mystic. Find your center. Nourish your inner light. That, too, is its own kind of magic-making, its own way of helping an anxious world find comfort, healing, and calm.

THE NINE OF CUPS REVERSED

It's easy to make a list of everything
you don't have. Everything you wished
was yours. That only feeds the fear
that you aren't enough. That the home
you crafted from the head of a dandelion
and a lifetime of elbow grease
is nothing more substantial
than one of those fairytale straw-houses
gone with one puff of wind. Silliness!
Don't you know that dandelions are
built to survive—thrive?
So why not make your home in them.

INSIGHTS

Ooohhhh... this was yet another lovely, hopeful card in the midst of so much upheaval. But then again, I was coming to see all cards in the tarot as hopeful in their own way. They are here to guide us, after all, and provide insight into what we are going through on this earthly plane.

When the Nine of Cups reversed enters your life, it's asking you to reconsider what makes you happy—and what is truly important to you. This is a great time to reevaluate your priorities when this card speaks to you (and as so many of us did during the pandemic). What are you focusing your time and energy on? Is it meaningful? Or is it merely something that has you spinning your wheels? Use this time to get rid of energetic riffraff and allow yourself to sink deeper into your inner wisdom.

It's also time to let go of any feelings of fear or insecurity that make you feel like you have to hold on to each and every material object to feel secure. Trust that you have enough, and that you are doing all you can. Oh, and one more thing: Beware of overdoing it. You're allowed to take time for yourself and your family right now. Resist the temptation to carry the world on your shoulders or fret over everything. It is enough to do your part and then enjoy the process of letting go of what no longer serves you.

DEATH REVERSED

I have a devil inside of me
that wants me spread
so thin, I'm a ghost of a thing. Thin
is so very fashionable after all—
and easily consumed.
I'd rather be my own morning star
and find my center in the earth's center.
There I am home among ancient roots
and dark quiet spaces that hold me
close. They know I am a luminous
seed that only needs stillness—
that fertile soil—to birth a new dawn within.

INSIGHTS

I love the Death card. Like the Devil—the card and the archetype—it's one of the most misunderstood figures. We've all seen that B horror movie with an ominous tarot reading that includes the Death card right before things get spooky. Well, guess what? The tarot isn't usually that literal! The Death card is all about transformation—shedding the past, moving on, and discovering ways to live more deeply, in tune with your truest self. Terrifying! Reclaiming your power always is, especially when the change is of a permanent nature, as this card implies.

Reversed, as it is here, things get a little tricky. Death reversed asks you to confront the areas in your life where you are resisting change. You might be feeling stagnant or fearful about what might happen if you take that leap of faith because, let's face it, change is scary. That's probably why this card has such a bad reputation. You know changes need to be made, but sometimes the idea of stepping into the unknown can be so terrifying we'd rather stay in the safety of nostalgia and The Good Old Days (which, if you're honest, weren't always as great as you liked to think they were).

Take, for example, our stay-at-home life during the pandemic. It might be easy to want to return to the way things were, but the reality is we never can—and never should. We should evolve. Take the good with us (compassion, empathy, relationality), and let go of the bad (mindless consumerism, busy addiction). We had the power to change our story, and Death reversed reminded us to have courage and do it.

Here's the juicy secret of this card: Sometimes it lets you know that you are in the midst of a transformation so deep, so profound, that you have no words for it. You only feel it as a soft, glowing energy inside you. This is a private thing, best processed and nourished in solitude. Honor your quiet sanctuary here and the space you have for cosmic revelations.

THE EIGHT OF SWORDS UPRIGHT

We become the stories
we tell about ourselves. I
once was a gravedigger,
before I realized I
was a gardener, planting
seeds instead of souls.
Funny, how changing
one word brings new life. I
once was a damsel
too, before I took up the sword.
I'm much better as the carver of new paths
than I ever was as a silenced woman.
My sword looks much like a pen
now. I wonder what story it will tell next.

INSIGHTS

Like many of the tough love cards of the deck, the Eight of Swords might seem like doom and gloom upfront, but its message is one of pure hope. This card is all about taking your power back and remembering that you have agency. It's hard not to get sucked into the fear and panic when life throws you plot twists, but this card asks you to do just that.

We see the figure at the center, bound and blindfolded, apparently trapped. But the truth is she could easily free herself if she takes her power back. There are plenty of swords to cut her ties loose and a castle in the distance where she can find refuge. She just has to stop feeding her fears or her sense of powerlessness. She literally has everything she needs to free herself right in front of her if only she can see it. When we find ourselves in troubling times, it's easy to fall into hysteria, allowing old ghosts and anxieties to flare up and feeding new ones. But none of that does a lick of good. You know what does? Being proactive, doing your part, and then bypassing the collective heebie-jeebies. Don't get sucked into doom and gloom. Instead, take your power back. It's right there in front of you.

THE MAGICIAN UPRIGHT

I've always been the practical
sort. Magic is only common sense,
after all—can't you see it
at my fingertips? It's what happens when I
ruthlessly toss mediocre prose
and dead ends into my compost—
fertile grounds for a more satisfying story. I
coax dreams into the waking world, sparks
of inspiration made flesh and blood beings
by my hand. I've crafted so many spells—
a whole book's worth—with more to come.
See what I mean? Magic.

INSIGHTS

If there were one card in the tarot deck that I'd choose to embody everyday magic, it would be the Magician. He is the quintessential occultist, well-versed in mysticism and the unseen world. But he's also a pragmatist who won't rely on smoke and mirrors to con his way into "magical" answers like some common charlatan. He knows that the magic comes from hard work. Lessons learned the hard way. A devotion to studying every aspect of the thing he wishes to know more about. It is simply in his nature to seek out knowledge—both worldly and otherworldly—and then carve his own path with the wisdom he's gained. He's a pragmatic idealist, an alchemical realist, a mundane mystic. In other words: He's my kind of guy.

When the Magician shows up in your life, it brings the promise of hard-earned success. Think of him as the master manifester. He's got all the belief it takes to dream big dreams, along with the elbow grease and knowledge to make them happen. He tells you that you are at the right place at the right time and that you're the one that's brought you to this point. This is a supreme empowerment card, meant to remind you that you are magic.

What you've accomplished so far might look to others like it has just fallen into your lap "like magic," but in reality, you've channeled the pragmatic energy of this card to make your dreams come true and honored your intuition that has guided you toward your chosen path. Like the figure in this card, you know that you must be in sync with your inner world, the Universe, and the outer world in order to conjure your specific brand of magic. You've got all the resources you need (notice the table full of occult tools in the card, echoing each suit in the tarot), plus the hard-earned knowledge to make it happen. So, what are you waiting for? Go make some magic.

STRENGTH UPRIGHT

I'm as fierce as a ladybug.
Nothing gets past my armored wings, except
the spring breeze that carries me
to the next flower. My roar is as terrifying
as a whisper in the dark. I've befriended
lions too—many of them. They're not so scary
when you know it's only an open
ear and a soft touch that they want. We're all wild things,
after all, wanting to be understood. We're all
wild things wanting to go untamed.

INSIGHTS

Here is a card that redefines strength. Traditionally in a patriarchal world, strength is depicted as brute force and extroverted action. But in the tarot, strength is a quiet, feminine thing regardless of your gender orientation. See how the woman in Strength caresses the lion's head and puts him at ease? She isn't trying to control him. Instead, they are two kindred spirits soothing and soothed by one another's presence.

When this card walks into your life, it's asking you to trust your wild heart and nourish your natural instincts. They will lead you where you need to go. Don't let self-doubt and fear be like a wild beast inside you. Trust your inner strength and move forward, knowing that you will outgrow those fears as you stick to your path. Likewise, don't dive into every conflict as a warrior. Sometimes the best path toward a resolution is a gentle touch.

This kind of deep, internal strength is something that needs to be actively cultivated. The more you trust it, the more you tend it, the stronger you get so that your personal power becomes a steady, grounding force. Let your strength be a quiet, wild animal. It won't need to roar and claw to make things happen. It can just softly go about its business, at one with the forest and the mysteries therein.

THE TOWER UPRIGHT

I have no use for ivory towers. Let them crumble,
their bricks and mortar put to better use. Give
them to someone who doesn't understand the freedom
of the wild wood. May they find comfort in the rubble.
All that masonry did was keep me from myself. So said the lightning
that gifted me to the earth. I'd rather make my home
inside a hollyhock. She asks only that I
turn my face toward the sun with her.

INSIGHTS

There are no two ways about it, The Tower is one of the most feared cards in the tarot deck and for good reason. Breakthroughs, transformations, and mind-blowing epiphanies can be terrifying! See the lightning striking the seemingly safe and sturdy tower, throwing its inhabitants to the earth? It's the end of the world! But in a good way.

This card is about getting grounded or "down to earth" like the figures jumping from the tower. And, even better, the lightning bolt of insight only destroys what needs to go—old attitudes, bad habits, self-limiting beliefs. The tower is never as sturdy as it seems, and it only ever represents bad things that need to go. Take the pandemic. It only laid bare the problems of our current system of hyper-consumerism, bad politics, mindless busy-ness, and dehumanization. It's scary, true, in part because we also have to confront our own complicity in these situations. But it is also extremely liberating to be free from the tower in which we willingly locked ourselves. The fact is, we've needed to free ourselves from unhealthy ways of being for a long time.

This also works on a deeply personal level as well. Sometimes you knowingly or unknowingly lock yourselves in a tower of your own making. You do it to survive, and you do it because you think it keeps you safe. You are both the evil witch and Rapunzel here, keeping yourself from the world and yet searching for escape.

Think of all the ways you've internalized what I call Ivory Tower Syndrome—white elitism, toxic patriarchy, impostor syndrome, extroverted performativity, and anything else designed to keep you down—and let it go. Visualize each stone in the tower as it breaks and crumbles. Then let yourself be free. When this card walks into your life, it asks you to embrace this radical transformation instead of fighting it. Get grounded and really think about what fulfills and heals you. Get rid of everything else.

THE THREE OF PENTACLES UPRIGHT

I've spent many years learning
how to coax a narrative from feathers,
half-remembered dreams,
and a handful of grit. I've spent even longer
learning the shape of a novel, from cover
corners to climax. So many hours and minutes and seconds
devoted to the words—worlds—kept inside paperbacks. I
don't know myself outside these stories. I think I'm just beginning
to understand what it means to be a story—
And how to write a good one.

INSIGHTS

Clearly, I wasn't done with the medicine of the Three of Pentacles, as it found its way back into my deck as I shuffled for this project. Only instead of a reversal, I got the card upright. I was right side up again, free from the burdens of meaningless work, but also still learning the art of mastering my craft.

Several years ago, I started my blog, *Enchantment Learning & Living*, to rediscover everyday magic and my writing voice. I wrote every day for a year. I wrote good stuff. I wrote bad stuff. I wrote forgettable stuff and stuff so memorable and magical that I turned it into a book. Before that, I wrote a lot of other stuff—a dissertation, a handful of half-written, semi-abandoned novels and short stories, and more essays than I can ever remember. Some of those things I'm proud of. I'm incredibly glad others will never see the light of day, and I happily consign them to my literary compost where they will nourish new—and better—stories. I've spent even longer being a voracious reader. After a lifetime of reading and almost as long writing, I'm just starting to get a sense of what makes a good story—and how to write one. When this card shows up, it asks you to enjoy the learning process. Don't rush or push or expect easy answers. Embrace the mess, the trial and error. The sweet epiphanies and the stunning plot twists. This card asks you to let your passion fuel you, let your calling be an act of devotion rather than an act of toil. Make the work you do meaningful, the relationships you develop full of productive magic.

Here's the thing about all those years of reading and writing that brought me here: I wouldn't have it any other way. I read because I had to. Stories nourished and informed me like nothing else. I wrote—again because I had to. It's no joke when I say that writing is an integral part of my self-care practice. I do it to heal, to explore, to dream. The Three of Pentacles tells me that I'm right on track with my proverbial apprenticeship. Maybe in another ten years, I'll have a better sense of what a good story looks like—both lived and written.

THE SEVEN OF WANDS UPRIGHT

Do you remember when the mountain
you now stand on was nothing but a jagged
outline on the horizon? Now you have roots
on that high ground. Now
you see the city spread out before you, the sky
stretching into the beyond. Not many get that view—
not many are willing to risk the climb
into the heavens. Here you have a home, a book, a garden—
and the promise of someone to share it with. See? Heaven.

INSIGHTS

Now here's an interesting card. The figure in its center looks ready to fight. He's on a mountain top, looking down at whatever threat is coming his way. He's also wearing two different types of shoes! The Seven of Wands, however, is less about going into battle, and more about living with integrity and staying strong in who you are. Those mismatched shoes? A symbol of doing things your own way. I mean, most people wear matching shoes, and when you don't, they might think it's because you're rejecting them and their life choices. In reality, you're just doing you. This card asks you to keep doing that—following your own heart, sticking to your guns, and living with integrity.

See the ease with which the figure holds his ground? Sometimes this is as simple as knowing who you are and celebrating your inner truth. When this card pops up, it asks you to resist the urge to conform or play nice to placate the masses. It's more important to stand firmly for what you believe in and do what is right for you.

THE TEN OF SWORDS UPRIGHT

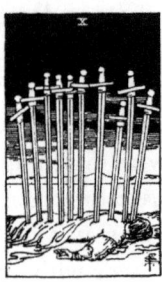

I've been taught to fear the unnamed
thing. The insidious whisper
that tells me I'm not enough. That my story
will be a sad one. That I must suffer
for every ounce of joy I bring into this world—
you see? My mind can be monstrous too.
You wouldn't believe the ugly futures it feeds
when tiredness sets in. But I'm not afraid
to name them. Let them fade with sunrise—
they are no match for my light.

INSIGHTS

Okay, I admit, this card does look pretty bad. But this is the tarot, and we must remember to read the card with more than a little bit of poetic license. The Ten of Swords is meant to shock you out of complacency, like a good horror story. It's over-the-top terrifying so that you will pay attention to the things you're too afraid to look at. And just like with a good supernatural tale, the terror of the card isn't the fact that the figure has been stabbed in the back by ten long, sharp swords. The terror is in the unknown. Who or what did that to him? Why wasn't he able to outrun it?

The fact of the matter is that it wasn't the unknown or the swords that did the figure in. It was the fact that he never stopped running to face what he needed to face. If we don't stop and take a good, hard look at the things we're most afraid of, they'll eat us up inside or cut us up, like ten swords through his back. Fears are like that. They grow more powerful in the darkness and unseen spaces of our minds.

Let's go back to the horror story analogy: What's scarier, the chill along your spine, and the whisper of something right behind you, or the monster in full view? Sure, the monster might be scary, but once you see it for what it is, it becomes less terrifying than all the unspoken possibilities of what it *could* be. That's the power of imagination. It can feed your self-doubt until you conjure a monster of your own making.

Here's some more poetic wisdom from the tarot: surrender. Sure, surrendering can be scary—it means losing control, letting go of the narrow life you've mapped for yourself, and being brave enough to stare down the thing you are most afraid of. But it's so worth it. You are allowed to be more than your deepest fears. In the place of phantom menaces, you have empowerment, catharsis, and hope. See what I mean? Just like a good horror story.

THE FOUR OF SWORDS UPRIGHT

I do my best work when I'm dreaming.
When the stillness breeds sunflowers,
and my solitude connects me to worlds
within words. You would be surprised
by what you discover when you
pause to converse with ladybugs or let your heartbeat
sync with the song of the Universe.
When your mind quiets so paperback
wisdom can speak. This truth they gift me:
I'm the sunrise before the world
is conscious. The songbird full of bronze notes—
magic awakening.

INSIGHTS

What a lovely second-to-last card to get at the end of my Tarot Tuesday journey, which started over two years ago. It's also a deliciously sweet card that asks us to cool off, unplug, and get grounded—a perfect antidote to everything that was going on in the world at the time.

The Four of Swords asks you to restore your inner peace. Solitude and quiet time are essential as you regroup and think about your priorities. In bruja terms, this card is about recharging and reclaiming your magic, your right to healing and self-care, your right to work quietly and consistently on bringing positive energy into your life and your communities.

We forget that stillness can be a form of action. Contemplation a powerful force. We start moving too fast, living too loud, and we forget to listen, to learn, to tune in to the wisdom that can only be found when we let go of the noise and distractions. Answers can always be found by turning inward. This doesn't mean that we ignore all that is going on in the world. It just means that we pause to find more meaningful ways of continuing the work that needs to be done. Reversed or upright, the card speaks to a profound need for self-care and nourishment at the deepest levels.

THE EMPRESS UPRIGHT

I remember when there was only fertile
soil at my feet and a half-dreamed hope—
one I planted, eternally optimistic
though there was little to make me so. I
got corn and beans and more herbs
than I can name from that one seed. Look
at the crops that came from a tender
heart! Look at the life I made from choosing wild living
things. We are one—earth, plant, body. Desert
heart beating despite the heat.

INSIGHTS

Wow. I'd made it! Over two years later... I finished my Tarot Tuesday project. And what a completely lovely card to end on. The Empress is goddess energy incarnate. She is Mother Earth. The divine feminine. Abundance manifested. She is all about the feminine energy, regardless of your gender, and all about nurturing the soft, creative fertility the traditionally female spirit embodies. Look at her in her garden, surrounded by the harvest she has lovingly tended. Fulfillment, she tells us, is in taking a moment to pause and feel gratitude for all you have done. Your dreams are now coming to fruition, and it is important to honor the work you've done to birth them.

When this card calls to you, it can signal that you might not be seeing the everyday magic all around you. Disconnection and burnout might feel like constant companions for you right now. This card reminds us, however, that there is hope, hope that can be found in deep, meaningful connections that transform lives and communities.

The Empress doesn't do things by halves. All her relationships—with the earth, self, and others—are deep connections that heal and nourish through human empathy and understanding. See her heart-shaped shield with the Venus symbol in it? She is the warrior of love. Self-love keeps her boundaries strong and the riffraff out. Her shield also protects those she loves, like sunshine ensuring that plants can grow and thrive. See the big picture, she reminds us, just like The Star. Remember that there is much power in the divine feminine and the interconnectedness she represents. We can heal the earth by healing our relationships to it and to one another. We can restore balance. We can obliterate anything that doesn't stand for love, inclusion, and healing.

CONCLUSION

Thank you for taking the time to converse with me and the tarot (and my familiar—that little black cat is hovering over my laptop as I type this). If you're looking to begin your own tarot studies or just develop them further, below are a few resources that I leaned on heavily while working on this project.

I'm indebted to *Wildly Tarot*, a wonderful podcast run by Holly Adams Easley and Esther Joy Archer, that does a great job of discussing the tarot, tarot readings, and various tarot decks. Their recent publication, *The History of Tarot Art: Demystifying the Art & Arcana, Deck by Deck*, is also a book I'm finding a lot of nourishment from as I continue my tarot studies. I learned quite a bit from Brigit Esselmont's *Biddy Tarot* website and her book, *Intuitive Tarot: 31 Days to Learn to Read Tarot Cards and Develop Your Intuition*. I also love Michelle Tea's *Modern Tarot: Connecting with Your Higher Self through the Wisdom of the Cards* and Jessa Crispin's *The Creative Tarot: A Modern Guide to an Inspired Life*.

Recently, I've started Benebell Wen's *Holistic Tarot: An Integrative Approach to Using Tarot for Personal Growth* and Helen Farley's *A Cultural History of Tarot*. These resources don't represent a definitive or even comprehensive guide to understanding the tarot, but they are all books that spoke to me as I began my explorations and as I continue to study the tarot. They came to me synchronously and resonated with my approach to everyday magic. May they bring you similar wisdom!

As for tips to get started in your own tarot reading journey, I would recommend first finding a deck that resonates with you. There are a lot of them out there! Take your time exploring and see what emerges. Remember, you do not have to wait to be gifted one. My only caveat to finding your deck is to make sure to check up on the artist and publisher background. As with all things related to the magical and witchy world, it's important to stay away from cultural appropriation or decks that lift heavily from cultures or groups with historically marginalized identities but are designed by artists with no real connection to those communities. Luckily, a little research will save you from purchasing any dodgy decks. I've had great luck with indie artists.

Once you have your deck, spend some time sifting through it, just looking at the various cards and admiring the art, with no specific agenda. Flip through the companion book and just linger over the vibe. Think of it as a casual first date with your deck that's low-key, no pressure, just feeling things out. From there, I would recommend daily tarot pulls, or weekly, if daily feels too much. Basically, get in the habit of shuffling and drawing a card regularly and learn its message. Don't get too hung up if you can't always remember what each card means—you'll gradually learn them through repetition and practice.

As you get used to your tarot routine, pay attention to patterns, like a series of reversals or suits, synchronous happenings in your life related to your readings, and what card or cards continue to speak to you. Do you keep pulling the same card over and over again? It still has medicine for you! Do you find one card that deeply resonates with you? That's the card that you share a natural affinity with—spend time exploring the nuances of it.

There are some pretty basic tips to keep in mind too. Things that seem pretty simple but are sometimes harder to pull off in real life: Don't consult the deck when you're upset or overly emotional. Easy to say until you're in upheaval and needing some advice! Seriously though, take a step back and a deep breath, then consult the deck and really listen to what it has to say. Don't ask too many questions at once—you'll get too many answers or too few. My favorite approach to readings is simply to shuffle and think about my day or situation or feeling as I do. Then I let the tarot comment on it, rather than asking for a specific question. This is a great way to consult the deck when you want advice but you aren't sure what to ask. And, this probably goes without saying, but once the tarot has spoken, don't try to pull new cards for the same question or issue right away, a common desire if you pull cards you don't like. The tarot will literally shut down and get all mystic-cryptic on you. It does not like to repeat itself. Trying a few weeks later to check on the progress of a situation? Sure. Just don't get obsessive. And really follow the advice the tarot offers—it will stop speaking to you if you ignore it and open up to you more if it knows you're really listening.

Lastly, once you get more comfortable knowing the basic meaning of each card, allow yourself to explore how *you* read the tarot. What type of reading styles resonate with you most? Do you like reading reversals? Not everyone does, but I find them incredibly helpful. Trust your own instincts as you allow the meaning of the cards to change, especially within the context of your questions and what's going on in your life. The card meanings can change over time, or put more deeply, we understand them better. Like people, they contain multitudes, so to limit them to one rigid interpretation, even if it's the one we start out with, likewise limits a more expansive reading of the deck. Better to relish the interpretive possibilities that unfold as you learn to read your deck.

Looking at *Conversations with the Tarot* holistically, I find it is such a joy to see where it started with the Ace of Wands, the magic of new beginnings, and where it ended with The Empress and her infinite ability to both enjoy and tend her abundant garden. Seems to me the perfect metaphor for our journey into tarot: We start with a seed, a spark, a burst of inspiration, and then steadily tend it until we've cultivated a mystical oasis, an enchanted haven, a delightful conversation that nourishes the magic of everyday life.

ABOUT THE AUTHOR

Dr. Maria DeBlassie is a native New Mexican mestiza and award-winning writer and educator living in the Land of Enchantment. She writes and teaches about spooky stuff, romance, and all things witchy. She is forever looking for magic in her life and always finding more than she thought was there. Find out more about Maria and conjuring everyday magic at mariadeblassie.com.

www.ingramcontent.com/pod-product-compliance
Lightning Source LLC
LaVergne TN
LVHW041219080426
835508LV00011B/1005